5

TITANIA'S NUMBER 5

Titania Hardie

For Georgia, my husband, and my second-born

A CONNECTIONS EDITION
This edition published in Great Britain in 2007 by
Connections Book Publishing Limited
St Chad's House, 148 King's Cross Road, London WC1X 9DH
www.connections-publishing.com

British Library Cataloguing-in-Publication data available on request.

ISBN 978-1-85906-227-2

1 3 5 7 9 10 8 6 4 2

Phototypeset in Bliss and Natural Script using QuarkXPress on Apple Macintosh
Printed in China

Contents

STARTING THE JOURNEY

This little book of numerology invites you to be amazed by what you will learn from numbers – about your character, your tastes, your instincts, your relationships, and even about your future. But to do this involves a willingness to believe – as Pythagoras, the 'Father of Numbers' did – that numbers can provide a clue, or formula, through which we can perceive some of the evolving patterns and cycles that affect our own individual existence. Let's find out more ...

Discovering numerology

Fans of Sudoku will understand how it entices us intellectually to see how strands of numbers – almost magically – slot together and interconnect with one another, revealing a rhythm of harmonious relationships between the lines. In one sense, numerology does this for us on a personal and spiritual level. The Science of Numbers, as it is called, suggests that there is an order and a rhythm in the universe of which we are a part, and although there is a certain mystery in the way numbers seem to function as symbols for our experiences, there is a long tradition across many cultures of their fascination for us.

Now, in an age of gigabytes, PINs and mathematic-based technology, how can we doubt the role that numbers play, or the way in which they have become part of our daily landscape? Numbers speak to us every day about our personal identity on this planet. Our birth date is absorbed by society as proof of our existence: you need it to be 'real' at the bank, in the office, when you travel, in an automated phone queue – in *all* official records. Indeed, many people consider the day-date of their birthday to be their lucky number. But can it really say anything about us?

Did you know, for instance, that:

- If you were a **1**, you'd rush off into any adventure and worry about it later; or if you were a **9**, you'd need to invest in good-quality luggage because you'd be bound to notch up a lot of air miles?
- Or that a **6** feels compelled to generously host open-house for guests and family?
- A **7** will want to specialize in whatever interests them?
- And an **8** would rather have one small quality gift than half a dozen less luxurious presents?

- Or that any friend who's a **4** will painstakingly spend hours getting something just right, whereas a **3** will have several projects on the go at one time and get through as best they can? C'est la vie!

But you've picked *this* little volume because you're a **5**, which means you should always try to maintain significant personal freedom in your life and career, and work independently for the public, if possible ... whereas if you had been a **2**, a partnership would be far better suited to your personality.

About this book

Each individual title in this series investigates, in depth, the meaning of one of nine personal numbers. *This* volume is dedicated to the exploration of the number **5**.

We will be focusing principally on your DAY number –

that is, the number relating to the day of the month on which you were born (in your case, the 5th, 14th or 23rd of the month). Calculating your **DAY** number is easy: you simply add the digits of your day together (where applicable), and keep adding them until they reduce to a single number (*see calculation examples on page 270*). And that's it. It doesn't matter which month or year you were born in – you just need the day-date to discover your **DAY** number. And *you're* a **5.**

Your **DAY** number reveals all kinds of information, and, working from this number, we will be considering:

- The obvious attributes of your number as they impact on your personality
- How you are likely to dress, and what colours or styles appeal
- How you react to things psychologically, and what drives or motivates you

- What annoys you most
- In which fields you will have the most natural abilities and gifts
- What sort of lover you are, and how you relate to all other numbers
- What the future holds

... and much, much more.

And you have another significant number too: your **LIFE** number. This is derived from adding up the digits in the *whole* of your birth date – day, month and year (*see examples on page 270*). What does *this* number mean, and what do your **DAY** and **LIFE** numbers mean in tandem? And how does it affect you if you're also a 'master' number (**11** or **22**)? Read on and you'll see. But first, let's meet your **DAY** number ...

So, you're a 5

5

You are one of the **adventurers** and gamblers of the world. Security is not important to you: your number is a byword for **versatility**, physicality and progress. You are sensuous and a **good communicator** – though perhaps restless and chaotic if forced into boring routine or menial tasks. This number is for living life to the full *each day*. And if you also happen to have a large number of 'E's, 'N's or 'W's in your name (each of which has a numerical value of **5** – more about which shortly), these **restless** qualities will be especially pronounced. You love danger, preferring to do things with gusto and **flair**.

All **5**s strive to adapt their **multifaceted** personality to any occasion, and must learn to complete the tasks they are given before heading off in a different direction –

leaving unfinished business, astonished spouses, or cranky colleagues or bosses in their wake. Of all the numbers, **5**s need a **second in command** – a sous chef, or a patient **4**, to complete the work at hand.

Number **5** implies **sexuality** and luxury to excess. You have a **mercurial essence**, the ability to tackle more than one task at a time, which can result in having too many irons in the fire. If you've had a broad education, you'll **amaze** others with the extent of your capabilities, and sheer variety of conversation topics and interests. **5**s demand answers to many questions, aware that **knowledge** is power. But the need for challenges and physical outlets can provoke the negative characteristics of **irresponsibility**, tantrums based on frustration, or total **unawareness** of the thoughts and feelings of others, and consequently family and friends may suffer disappointment, heartache or feelings of chaos. As a **5**, however, you are prone to complete **mood changes** during the course of a conversation, allowing you to walk away from any relationship without a backwards glance. This is the 'guillotine effect'.

You have the **resourceful** qualities to make the necessary changes in life, whether it's your sales ability for a new idea or product, your **unconventional** approach to a business plan, or your **expansive** attitude to any new direction. If you present your ideas in person it is *very* difficult to refuse you. The **5**'s love of change and movement stimulates you to greater heights and prolific productivity.

5s get **impatient** easily, dislike the mundane, and hate to be held back or fenced in, as you are **investigative**, fun-loving, free-thinking, **gregarious** and unprejudiced. Very **physical**, you enjoy being popular with the opposite sex, and are sometimes an opportunist. Stylish and talented in numerous ways, you are a capable **interpreter** – if not with languages, then with the needs of the public. You dress distinctively, often seductively or dashingly (*especially* the men), using your **imagination** and magnetism to achieve the desired effect. And the next day may see a different look; change is *almost* as good as a holiday for you.

At best, **5**s are **original** and **dynamic**, but you can be arbitrary, **bizarre** and careless or **contrary** towards others, and should be ready to recognize that, on your more ungenerous days – when you feel thwarted by others who think more cautiously – you can be **uncontrollable** and erratic. You will best influence peers and loved ones when you are adaptable – or at least amicable: you must sometimes slow down and be patient, and be willing to go over your plans with those who don't see an end result happening as quickly or as clearly as you do.

You need variety, excitement and **stimulation**, and love to travel. A **risk-taker**, you should ideally work either in your own business, or as a consultant, allowing you **freedom** within your chosen role. If you have an extra helping of **5**'s characteristics, you'll be more extravagant, possibly eccentric, and definitely **progressive**. You are the 'it girl/guy' with the must-have gimmicks, sensing how a trend will develop – though you can be *too* ahead of the game! It's all down to timing, as you have enormous talent for progressing ideas. Your quick, **inquisitive** mind allows you to utilize information and see the new direction for others. You express ideas with verve, and are **articulate** on various subjects. Avoid being contrary and erratic and you will always **impress** those who look up to you.

Sound familiar? Getting a taste for what your number is about? And this is just the beginning. You'll soon find out how the number 5 expresses itself as your Day number in each and every day of your life. But before we go any further, let's take a look at where all this first came from ...

What's in a number?

Numbers have always had a sacred meaning. The Egyptians used an alphabet that conflated letters and numbers, and, as such, each number exuded an idea that was more than the sum it stood for. There is a whole book of the Old Testament devoted to the subject; and the Hebrew language – exactly like the Egyptian – has a magical subtext of meaning where letters and numbers can be doubled to reveal an extra layer of secret, so-called 'occult' information. It is called the *gematria*, and forms a crucial part of the sacred occult wisdom called Kabbalah. There were twenty-two letters – a master number – in both the Greek (Phoenician) and Hebrew alphabets, and repetitions of the spiritual properties of the numbers **3** and, especially, **7** recur throughout the Bible.

The Father of Numbers

But modern numerology derives more formally from Pythagoras, the Father of Numbers, who was a serious and spiritual philosopher, as well as the man who explained some of the secrets of geometry. Born on the island of Samos, although he ultimately settled in Cretona, a Greek colony in southern Italy, he is understood to have travelled widely to both Egypt and Judea. Some accounts of his life also suggest he may have studied under the Persian sages of Zoroaster, but an analysis of his teachings certainly reveals the strong influence of Kabbalistic thought in his philosophy.

Pythagoras understood numbers as a *quality* of being, as well as a *quantity* of material value. In one sense, the numbers as figures were connected with the measuring of things, but 'number' itself was significantly different to this, and encompassed a spiritual value. The numbers from one through to nine represented universal principles through which everything evolves, symbolizing even the stages an idea passes through before it becomes a reality. Mathematics was the tool through which we could apprehend the Creation, the universe, and ourselves. Musical harmony was a sacred part of this knowledge, as was geometry, which revealed divine proportion.

Most importantly, Pythagoras believed that numbers were expressive of the principles of all real existence – that numbers themselves embodied the principles of our dawning awareness, our conjecture and growth. Through mathematics and number we could approach divine wisdom and the workings of the universe as a macrocosm. Thus, in microcosm, our personal 'mathematics' would unlock the workings of our own being, and help us to see a divine wisdom concerning ourselves. **1** was not just the first digit, but also had a character of beginning, of independence, of leadership, just as the number **2** was more than merely the second number quantifying two objects, but also implied the philosophical concept of a pair, of co-operation, of a relationship beyond the individual.

Pythagoras also believed that we could understand our direction and fate through an awareness of repeating cycles of number, making numerology a key to revealing our opportunities and our destiny.

By tradition, the doctrine Pythagoras taught to his students in the sixth century BCE was secret, and no one wrote down his ideas until his death. But Plato was a follower of Pythagoras and, along with the rebirth of Platonism, the ideas of the Father of Mathematics were revealed afresh during the revival of Greek learning in the Renaissance. The great magi of the fifteenth and sixteenth centuries explored anew the significance of number and the gematria, to understand the hidden messages of the ancients and of the divine mind. Mathematics as a philosophy was the bridge to higher realms of spirituality.

Essence of the numbers

one is the spark, the beginning, Alpha, the Ego of consciousness. It is male.

two is consort. Adding partnership, receptivity, it is female, bringing tact.

three is a synthesizing of both of these qualities and brings expansion and joy.

four is the number of the Earth, of the garden, and of stability. It brings order.

five is curiosity and experiment, freedom, changes. It brings sensuality.

six nurtures and cares for others. It will love and beautify, and brings counsel.

seven perfects and contemplates the Creation. It is intellect, stillness, spirit.

eight is the number of power, the octave, a higher incarnation. It brings judgement.

nine is humanity, selflessness, often impersonal and all-knowing. It brings compassion.

Applying the knowledge

A deeper understanding of the self can be achieved through an awareness of the mysticism of number within us; and both the birth date and, to some degree, our given name are the keys to unlocking our mystical, spiritual core of being. Exploring the affinity between letter and number can also reveal insights about the lessons we need to learn throughout our lives to improve and develop as individuals (*see page 25*).

This book looks at the significance of numbers as they affect us every day, focusing largely, as introduced earlier, on our **DAY** number. It is this number that reveals to us our instincts, our impulses, our natural tastes and undiluted responses, our talents and immediate inclinations. This is how people see us in daily situations, and how we behave by essence.

We will be exploring how our **DAY** number influences

our love relationships and friendships; at what it says about our career strengths and our childhood; at the way our number manifests in our leisure time; and at how it might give us a better understanding of what to expect in our future cycles, as we pass through any given year under the sway of a particular number. Each birthday initiates a new cycle, and each cycle seems uncannily connected with the philosophical concerns of the number which governs that year. Look both to the past and present to see how strongly the number-cycle can illuminate our experiences ... and then count ahead to ponder what may be in store over the next year or two.

And numbers also say something about where we live or work, about our car, and even about our pets. Understanding these secret qualities can add a new dimension of pleasure – not to mention surprise – to our journey through life.

A NUMBER TO GROW INTO

The presence of our **LIFE** number, however, takes longer for us to appreciate in ourselves – longer for us to grow into – and it often takes time to reveal itself. This number comes to the fore as your life progresses, and on pages 214–247 we will be looking at the meaning of your **DAY** number together with your individual **LIFE** number, to see what this reveals about your character and potentiality.

The **LIFE** number may intensify the experience of the **DAY** number – if it is closely related to it, or shares similar patterns. But more frequently our two different numbers clash a little, and this often allows insight into the aspects of our being where instinct pulls us in one direction but higher wisdom or experience mediates and pulls us in a second direction.

Who would have thought you could learn so much from a number? Pythagoras certainly did, over 2,500 years ago ... and now you will discover it too.

What's in a name?

Your name also has a story to tell, and it is a story revealed through number. Every letter corresponds to a number: in the Western alphabet we use twenty-six letters, which are at variance with the twenty-two formerly enshrined in the Hebrew and Greek alphabets. Some numerologists believe that this is in keeping with the more material world we now live in, as the number '26' reduces to '8' (when you add the digits), which is the number of power and money.

The correspondences between the numbers and the letters of the alphabet are as follows:

1	2	3	4	5	6	7	8	9
A	B	C	D	E	F	G	H	I
J	K	L	M	N	O	P	Q	R
S	T	U	V	W	X	Y	Z	

As you are a **5**, it is most revealing to look at the letters E, N and W as they occur (or not!) in your name. This is because they intensify the experience and impression of your main number.

To make the most of the qualities inherent in your number, you should be using a name which is in poetic harmony with your **DAY** number. As a **5**, you will exude the quicksilver-mind response to everything, which should enable you to seize opportunities and propel you into the progressive frontiers you were born to explore. Using a name which includes an E, N or W bolsters your powers. If this sounds strange, consider that many of us have our names shortened or played upon by friends, family and lovers, so it is important to feel that our chosen name – the one that we use as we go about in the world – is making the best of our abilities and energies.

Among the letters that are equivalent to the number **5**, E is a vowel – and a common one, at that – so the chances are that you have a letter E in your name. It is especially significant if your name starts with an E, for the vowels represent the soul in our name, and to begin a name with a vowel means the soul is very strong within the character. The first vowel in the name also carries extra significance, as this is where the soul is said to enter our spirit – so if your first vowel is an E, you have an extra dose of the adventurous and restless spirit, and immense physical strength, associated with the number **5**.

The letter-numbers help us to act out our sense of purpose, and if these work in correspondence with the **DAY** number we are more likely to find our sense of will and achieve our goals more rapidly. But if we have few, or none, of the letters of our **DAY** number, we often feel it is much harder to shine in our field of opportunity. Let's take a closer look at what this means ...

Missing a '5' letter?

As a **5**, you will find you reach your career potential more easily if your business name includes one of the above letters. However, as a **5**, living up to your character traits can be demanding. Your number desires freedom, and requires some training and self-discipline to ensure that this freedom is, at all times, *constructive*.

If your name lacks a '**5**' letter, you may feel that you are clear in your vision of what the world around you needs, or what you want to do to be fulfilled, yet that you struggle in finding the spontaneity and enterprising qualities normally so much a part of **5**'s character. Or, in social life, your natural wish to be gregarious, fun-loving and communicative may be jeopardized, if the name that you use is without one of these letters. Something as simple as varying the spelling of your name could change this, and mean that you learn how to assert your individuality and feel that you are being listened to. Get your peers and loved ones to give you a pet name to offset any imbalance.

Too many 'E's?

It can be just as much of a problem if your name carries a flood of letters which correspond to your number. This potentially gives you an overdose, and brings out some of the more negative qualities associated with **5**.

A lot of 'E's in the name you use can make you too careless, erratic, imprudent and insatiable, failing to relate decisively with others. You assume everyone is on your wavelength, when they actually have no idea what you are talking about! Equally, a name with many 'N's can make you either clever and dynamic, or apathetic and dull. Try to choose a name for everyday use which minimizes the number of '**5**' letters.

YOUR DAY NUMBER

It's a new day ...

You will learn a lot about the numbers of your birthday and your name as this book unfolds, but the DAY number is, to my mind, the most important – and sometimes least well-recognized – number of all ... the number which exerts a magnetic hold on us each and every day of our lives. Every time we react to a situation, an emotion, a provocation of any kind, we are shooting straight from the hip, as it were, and this reaction is coloured by our DAY number.

As we know, your 'Day Force', or day, number is **5** if you were born on the 5th, 14th or 23rd of any month. Each of these different dates also affects us – the characteristics of the number derived from a birthday on the 14th vary intriguingly from one on the 23rd, for instance – and we will look at these differences in the pages ahead.

All three dates, however, still reconcile to an overall **5**. This number determines your gut reactions and the way you express yourself when you are being most true to yourself. Your parents, lovers, friends and co-workers all know you best through this number.

So what is the theme of being a 5? What are you like when you're at work, rest and play? And how compatible are you with the other numbers? Let's find out ...

5'S CHARACTER

Charms, graces, warts and all ...

When a 5 baby arrives, there is a little torrent of energy unleashed in the world! Yours is the number of constructive freedom and progress, and it likes to change things from the first hour of its birth. With this DAY number you are a bundle of progressive energy waiting to burst on to the stage of life, and you should really only mix with 'birds of a feather', from the cradle to the grave. 5s don't understand inactivity or boundaries, and are always looking for a way out – whether over or *through* such obstacles. 5s are here to lead the public towards change – and hopefully that change is always for the better.

Free spirit

Your energy astonishes everyone, even those who know you well. You never have to be told something twice, having grasped the concept almost before the other person has finished their sentence, and you want to be involved in what is going on in this world. You like to push ahead in all areas, taking others with you on your journey; when you believe in a concept or course of action, there is no better person to invigorate the public to that end. The law, and the right way to go about things, is important to you. It's not unusual to find **5**s at the controls in the community, quite able to turn failure into success. **5**s are here to experience freedom at every level – free-thinking free spirits, free to move onward and upward, free to learn and free to love.

So what can't you abide? Dullness, plodding boredom, someone who can't let go, being stuck in the proverbial rut, a prison cell or solitary confinement, a nine-to-five job, 'twenty-four/seven' without room for improvement, feeling trapped, monotony ... You came into this world to facilitate change and take others with you toward opportunities and lasting growth. So get going – now!

By adulthood, **5**s are well acquainted with sudden and abrupt changes. Young **5**s often flit from interest to interest, lover to lover, job to job – the proverbial rolling stone, gathering naught along the way. They may facilitate and engineer upheavals, just to get things moving. This is an important learning curve, and the inability to stick to a chore and complete it will only bring disappointment and loss, until the need for personal discipline and application has been recognized and mastered. A **5** must *perfect* – step by step – attributes of application, stability, the laws of growth and harvest, personal dependability, self-discipline; and, above all, you must balance your bounty of experiences and talent, using practicality and emotional maturity, toward a creative and artistic career or life path.

Keynotes of the 5 personality

Positive associations: active, exuberant, gifted, flexible, alert, curious, broad-minded, creative, charming, dynamic, original, entertaining, intuitive, independent, resourceful, emancipated, witty, freedom-loving, sensuous, eager

Negative associations: apathetic, agitated, hysterical, impulsive, insatiable, negligent, extravagant, boring, fearful, doubtful, inactive, stagnant, over-indulgent, erratic, ineffective, wayward, unresponsive, contrary

Your public awaits!

Humour and wit bubble to the surface of the **5** personality, and you love centre stage, approval from work chums and – let us not forget! – the applause of the adoring audience. If you don't pursue a stage or screen career, you may be an entertaining after-dinner speaker or sought-after public speaker for business seminars. The ability to think on your feet and joust with words can bring financial opportunity or a political career, not to mention happy family functions or hilarious Christmas parties where you are ever the clown. Having the prime number for communication skills can lead you into the legal profession, or from thespian to theologian, door-to-door sales to online marketing ... In short, you can influence the public and 'sell coals to Newcastle', or preach to the converted!

5s preside in fashionable boutiques: the more unusual the line or item the better. Real estate salesperson, editor, writer, the diplomatic corps or the travel industry – all are possible paths to employment or investment. Because you are capable of multi-tasking (multi-everything, in fact!), the corporate world would equally benefit from your services.

But remember: if something seems too good to be true, then it *is* too good to be true! And, just in case you thought no one could outwit your salesmanship ... well, there's no bigger target than a great salesperson, so a **5** can fall the hardest into the 'fast net' of the confidence trickster! It is worth repeating, as a personal catechism, that there is no such thing as a free lunch: it's better to *invest* intelligently, rather than to speculate or gamble for a fast buck and a thrill. And, you must learn to accumulate and build toward a lasting success and personal *security*: **5**s have 'grease-lightening' hands, and money slips through them at a rate of knots. Yes, it's true that for your cash has so many places to go ... just like you. Wisdom may come later, at some personal cost.

You will find yourself giving advice to friends, work-mates, family members. **5**s excel at unravelling mysteries, being so pleased to be of service. On the other hand, you are happy to sit quietly, totally absorbed in reading a murder mystery or watching a travel documentary or crime scene investigation unravelling – having already solved the case yourself, of course. It is hard to keep surprises for **5**s!

Think before you speak ...

So, are there cautions, then, for your enterprising number? Absolutely! Stay out of courtroom battles through misunderstandings: take time to seek mediation or acknowledge impulsive reactions, or to communicate appreciation for others' talent and effort – and be aware that courtroom battles make lawyers very rich, waste time and cause both parties enormous stress and financial loss. In all situations, and in your relationships, there's a possibility you can self-destruct through your own nervous energy, and you need to recognize that you have this weakness and take measures to impede disaster. Think before you react, then think again before you speak – in fact, count to twenty before you speak or react unfavourably. You may have changed your view by the morning, in any case.

5 represents *constructive* change, not total destruction or disappointments that bring disaster and further humiliation. This impulsiveness – this need to be *doing* – is something that time will help you to reflect on. Yes, you're here to keep things moving forward, to take friends and colleagues into new spheres of accomplishment, to excite, promote, sell and convince, because you understand that for humanity to survive it must welcome change. **5** is ever ready to facilitate that change, but sometimes you must pause for a moment and consider the most pragmatic way to achieve that. Choosing a team who can accommodate your will and impatience – while addressing the significance of your mission – is obviously a crucial factor.

Thirst for knowledge

Though you never intend to disrupt people's lives or go to extremes, you are always restless, reactive, and on the move forward into the unknown, anxious to have the information *now* – to know exactly what is going on. This innate curiosity and insatiable quest for knowledge guarantees that life is far from dull. People are assets to you 'fast lane' **5**s, and variety is your spice in life!

Events throughout your life have probably made you think and act quickly – from the earliest age. With talent, personal energy and magnetism, the world seems to force you to develop and draw on these qualities. **5**s often miss out on an easy childhood and are forced to find their freedom early on; but, as you grow older and discover your adventurer's spirit and sense of wit, life should become easier. Then, perhaps, you are allowed to be properly young at heart. This is often true for **1**s as well, yet they are asked to be independent and stand alone, whereas you must constantly adapt to upheavals. The pattern of acting and instigating change, and of learning to be ready to move and travel, has been ingrained from the cradle.

Many people see you as impatient, brittle and scattered, restless or discontented, a person skimming over the surface of life. There is some truth in this, for you often put yourself in positions where you react moodily, behave erratically and speak out critically, especially when things aren't moving in the direction you desire, or if you are restricted and can't be useful. But aggressive speech and dissatisfaction is just as likely to be a defensive reflex and an attempt to disguise the irritation you may feel at delays or the need for repeated efforts by yourself and others.

Making a statement

The world sees you as 'wired' – and **5**s are indeed movers and shakers, but are usually moving too quickly to worry about whether or not the passers-by like what they see. Your number is the 'sensual adventurer', and you stand out from the crowd like a blazing beacon. You like to!

Your personal image is vital to what you do, and your style is signature. Female **5**s take note: low necklines may be unsuitable for the office, but you will take it to the edge of the wire. You often express yourself boldly in fashion terms: flimsy cocktail-party frivolities, or dresses or tops that are too flashy, will frequently lure the opposite (or same) sex, but they can harm your professional image, too, and allow others to write off your real ability. Exercise caution, and think twice about the occasion – though no one doubts your flair. It is ever your subconscious desire to excite and attract, and you may 'go where angels fear to tread'. Still, you are a **5**, and it's important that you present yourself well and represent your vibrant personality accurately. Although you have myriad personalities and moods, it would benefit you to get it right first time.

You love to challenge the rules that exist – or create new options. **5**s are independent thinkers who take action and won't allow anyone to hold them in check for any length of time. When young, you may have had difficulty keeping to the task, and perhaps study and application weren't your strong suits, despite your high intelligence. There were just too many things to learn and absorb, too many people to listen to and observe, too many boundaries to push. Your teachers, if you thought them dull or the topic uninteresting, will most likely have witnessed you becoming the 'class clown', and you probably set about injecting you own particular sense of humour to liven things up and cause disruptions and distractions. Yours would be the report card that read: 'If _____ concentrated on what is being taught in class, they could show real progress. This student needs to learn how to make *good use of time* – and not squander it.' A valuable lesson!

Trust in yourself

Perhaps the most important advice for a **5** concerns your approach to life. You already know that you're on a mission to be free from constraints, but it's in your interest to be seeking creative outlets through the arts, writing, pottery, theatre, sculpting, painting and design or public speaking. As the school report card said, you shouldn't squander your innate creativity on a restless search for material or physical satisfaction.

Many **5**s are blessed with bountiful talents, and your duty to yourself is to direct them. Take that childhood dream or interest, and rekindle it; reinvigorate the gift, put your energy into your talents and grow to be who you were born to be. Without true achievement, your sense of frustration will send you into a downward spiral often manifesting in physical ills, and it is no use blaming regulations or your superiors for any blockages to your progress. Don't forget that you are one of the most progressive people in this world, and that this does occasionally justify being contrary, moody and impatient. When your inspiration is high you are enlightened and wise, and you need to trust that sense of purpose.

You love to express yourself, and to help others enjoy all that life has to offer. Nevertheless, you can become a higher-minded human being if you acknowledge that other people have different needs, and they will appreciate your attempts to include them in your plans. No amount of praise for your versatility and superior talent, though, is an excuse for lapsing into total self-indulgence, or a justifiable reason for giving up and throwing the baby out with the bathwater, when conditions or plans go awry.

5s may run from one thing to another, unable to complete or commit without a thought as to the consequences for their employer or partner. Or, they might immerse themselves in a 'safe haven' – a desk job or marriage with many children and responsibilities, that ensures they lack room to move. Georgia, a close numerologist friend of mine who is a **5**, has dubbed this the 'saddle effect'. Whereas someone with a **DAY** number of **2** or **4**, or even **6**, would find such a situation blissful, a **5** allows it to momentarily delay progress, so they feel *saddled* with it. It becomes part of the excuse not to complete something.

There is no escaping your duty as a **5**, however, and the difficulties and changes you are due will simply surface in another form: insecurity, fear, boredom, irresponsibility – or in too much responsibility, and a consequent resentment of the load. Then you will feel stagnant, bored, ineffective and quite possibly unresponsive. But this is not your authentic self.

To conclude on an upward note, it is to your credit that most experiences will be a great teacher for you. You observe people and circumstances – and absorb what you see – and have a propensity for adventure and independence, for quick understanding and free-thinking. You will fit a great deal into your life, and rarely allow yourself to become negative for long. Dissatisfied with the old ways of doing things, you are a joy to have on board for anyone who looks to your enthusiasm and spontaneity to carry them into the future, or to turn failure into success.

You are inspirational and vibrant, electrical and tireless, physical and involved. You are, indeed, a venturesome, inventive individual, and this means you have what it takes to show the rest of us the non-conformist way forward.

5 in a nutshell

Personality watchwords: progressive, freedom-loving
Lucky colours: lilac, wisteria, cerise, claret, raspberry, pink
Lucky herbs/flowers: lavender, sandalwood, peppermint
Scents: lavender, sandalwood, peppermint, fig, olive
Fashion style: sensual, attention-getting, cleverly cut/designed, quality fabric, adaptable, easy to pack
Decorative style: open plan, clean lines, expansive view/ overlooking water, garden large enough for entertaining
Letters: E, N or W (needed in the name you use)
Car style: turbo-charged, zippy, convertible, Vespa
Holiday destination: 'action' holiday or African safari

Which 5 are you?

1 2 3 4 **5** 6 7 8 9

Everyone with a day number of **5** will exhibit many of the characteristics just discussed. It is interesting to see, though, how the number **5** varies across all of its incarnations. There is a subtle but definite difference between the way the number operates for someone born on the 5th of the month – which makes for a pure **5** effect – and someone born, say, on the 23rd.

As a rule, anyone born on the single-digit date has the truest and most undiluted effect from the number, whereas someone born as a product of two digits borrows some qualities from the pairing of the numbers. Twenty-anything puts the softening digit '2' before the second number, and this usually means that, whatever number you are, you are more aware of the needs of others. Similarly, if '1' is the first digit (14th), you are more independent and freedom-seeking, and perhaps more conscientious and assured of your self-worth than other **5** people.

Let's look at the variations across all the birthdays ...

Born on the 5th?

You're versatile, enthusiastic, amusing, entertaining, progressive, clever, imaginative and talented – but yet you may lack the patience you sometimes need to finish a job, and may be irritated by responsibilities. As someone who likes presenting ideas, has a clever and quick mind but loathes routine and the mundane, you prefer to leave back-up tasks to others, so delegating is less of a problem for you than for other **5**s.

You are restless and physically demonstrative, thrive on praise and affection and enjoy emotional and physical interaction. Capable of working long hours, you work well with other people, but you are not patient. You may be the most sociable, amusing and talented of the **5**s, but you often feel misunderstood by many who think you superficial. A survivor, you must do your best to rein in the excesses – wine, lovers, drugs, food ... At different times in your life various things will play a pivotal role, and there is little doubt that other people's lives will be affected.

With a special gift for freedom-fighting, you are convinced of your public duty. You adore acting, employing your charm, humour and gift of interpretation to entertain friends, family or captive audiences. You love to find things out, so would make a good detective; curious about life, you're an interesting conversationalist and witty debater.

Sexually, you may be either strangely abstinent, or unbridled, hedonistic, sensual and experimental; either way, sometimes *very* demanding. Perhaps you feel as though your physical need and expectations are as much a part of the daily functions of life as eating, sleeping and brushing your teeth. But you also know how to create romantic interludes, and are usually willing to do this to help rekindle the glow that is diminished when there is a daily demand for sexual intimacy.

Travel is vital to you, so your passport will be up-to-date and your quality luggage ever ready, because – like **9** – yours is the number of the frequent traveller. Short jaunts, cruises, day-trips, the big adventure to uncharted territory – you'll experience them all; a book on '100 places to visit before you die' is a must-read. You have a talent for any work connected with transportation, travel, sport and recreation and, perhaps not unrelated, tourism and real estate (sales and promotions). In fact, it's not unusual for you to work two or three jobs, juggling many demands.

Somehow shy, moody, soulful, and always looking for answers (the deeper meaning of life), it is not unusual to find you fascinated by spiritual, religious, metaphysical or occult studies. These interests lead you back to a fascination with the law and government policy, community services and land and environment services; these passions will be best supported by the numbers **2** and **4** anywhere else in your numbers (a predominance of the letters B and

T, or D and M in your name, for instance). The letters F, O or X in your name, in conjunction with your birthday, would bolster your natural facility with fashion, beauty and the other creative arts and services. But, whatever else, you need to work in an area that allows you the freedom to influence and progress humanity.

Because you are energetic and a multi-tasker, we should address your stress levels. You have quite possibly been living on the edge of nervous collapse. Living on your nerves becomes such a familiar state that you are unable to unravel your distresses. Let go of the high-tension wire and relax, meditate, detoxify (especially liver-cleanse!), and find a yoga class, or at least begin with a vigorous walk in the park or along the seafront. In all probability, this could lead you to a career in health care and fitness, or in wholefood outlets that support healthy eating and food preparation. You have a huge capacity to promote and advance humanity's desire for progress and fitness.

Born on the 14th?

Your birthday shares some similarities to the 1st, as it contains the pure digit '**1**' – and you are equally independent and self-reliant as someone born on the 1st, sometimes bossy (admit it!), and naturally assume the lead even in adverse circumstances. Plus the organized, cautious, conscientious practicalities of the **4** influence the way you express your desire for freedom, which is, at times, more self-protective. But you can also be more impulsive, which can lead you into destructive and frivolous behaviour.

Your energies and ideas are positively progressive, perhaps more spiritual and magnetic than the pure **5**, due to the presence of the **4**, which hates to see things destroyed. Good! This makes you more desirous of building and accumulating, of being law-abiding, and you're less likely to want to crash and burn. You are still vulnerable to physical burn-out, nervous exhaustion, ills and emotional stresses, though, and the caution is clear: you are better suited to less stressful pursuits such as the arts, music, writing, selling, PR, travelling and tourism, and areas where your freedom is not jeopardized or your ideas stifled.

You are extremely attractive to the opposite sex, and forceful in getting what you want – and can carry that attraction well into your senior years. Your mental energy and vitality will spark the mind and interests of many an admirer. But if you make physical attraction your motivator for relationships, don't expect them to be long-lasting; the same goes for money-based relationships – though you can rest assured that you will work hard, and earn every penny, for the duration of that involvement.

You are a contradiction emotionally, demanding personal freedoms yet requiring a stable, loving and emotionally communicative relationship in which to thrive. Just as there are two strong numbers in '14', there are two strong sides to you: charming and convincing, or combative and plain-speaking. You are drawn to all that is new, exciting, valuable and state-of-the-art; however, because you have the gambler's spirit and heart, heed the caution and set yourself boundaries, budgets, parameters and standards, for your excesses must be curtailed and self-discipline must be mastered. Fundamentally, your daily lesson is to learn not to scatter your energies. Focus and system must be developed, usually via the artistic fields: in this way, you are tapping into your immense creative talent.

The number 14 carries with it indebtedness, often called a Karmic Debt, for having mishandled freedom in a past incarnation, so that on this journey you will encounter the need to *repeat your effort* to achieve. 14 resonates to the freedom-loving, quick-moving **5**, so it is a daily challenge. Four numbers carry so-called Karmic Debt lessons and experiences: 13, 14, 16 and 19 (and some treat the numbers 11, 22, 29 and 33 as carrying indebtedness too).

Born on the 14th, you are motivated to welcome and initiate change, constantly move, travel and communicate, although you also encounter delays, obstacles, jealousies, and hesitancy to initiate action.

When we take the numbers apart, we look first to the number **1**, and, for the purpose of the karmic lesson, we consider its *negative* influences: selfishness, ego, dominance, temper, self-centred interests and a demanding nature. The negative influences of the **4** indicate inflexibility, irresponsibility, stubbornness, pessimism, lack of application, total disorganization, while the negative influences of the **5** – your **DAY** number – would result in the individual being scattered and ineffectual. As with all **5**s, beware of excesses – in this case, in any or all of the following areas: obsessive/compulsive tendencies, overeating, drinking too much, over-exercising, substance abuse, sexual frustrations. All can result in moral decay or over-consumerism. Your charm and determination is *paramount.*

Born on the 23rd?

With the marriage of the numbers **2** and **3**, you are perhaps more able to read and intuit others' needs than the pure **5** birthday. This date makes you a talented individual, and symbolizes a high degree of sensitivity, nervous tension, creativity and dexterity. You have a capacity for deep affection, once it has been bestowed on someone. This sets you apart from other **5**s, and the number **2** makes you considerate of your partner's needs. You are quite private and gentle, less confrontational and demanding in your desire for personal freedom, and able to fit versatility, charm and a variety of talents into your relationships more successfully than the other **5**s.

As **2** is feminine and has a non-confrontational manner, your relationships and friendships are sometimes quite unconventional. You love sincerely, but you will love whomever you will, with or without family approval! You are a 'chancer', a maker and taker of opportunities, and a charismatic partner. You start lots of projects and know when to delegate, so that other more suitable people may bring them to completion. This offsets the possibility that you will lose interest anyway, once things are up and running.

You are broad-minded yet sensitive to the essence of perfect timing, and can wait quite patiently until the time is ripe to propel yourself into action. Often, you might wait for opposition to evaporate or to tire, or simply to leave the office, for you to achieve your way, get the action you want, or put a plan into play. How many times you have lived to regret this? This happens because you miss the warning signals: if the sign says 'Stop! You're going the wrong way!', it's trying to warn you, asking you to stop, consider other options or choose a better time for action. Yes – you didn't see any such sign; but that is what the delays you encounter are all about. When the time is right, it will astonish you just how easily, how smoothly and perfectly the events you desire fall so beautifully into place.

It's possible that it may take you a while to build your confidence when starting an enterprise or launching out into a new direction, and you are more likely to speak boastfully about your progressive plans, while attempting too many tasks and leaving others unfinished. You frustrate workmates and bosses, who see you as unreliable, and this means that you may miss out entirely, having your hopes dashed, and suffering huge disappointment and dissatisfaction. But take heart, as the **2** in front of the all-creative **3** indicates that you are detailed, co-operative and able to place those 'little things' exactly where they belong, using facts and figures wisely. This is an innate talent.

You are an affable and enthusiastic spokesperson, asked to present and promote new projects. The **5** makes you prepared to expand and expound on the virtues of freedom, variety, change, people's rights and adventure; you can see that this would lead you into the legal profession, politics and theatrical pursuits, or the sales and travel industry. You are ready to assert your rights as well as those of others, but your **2** and **3** together in addition help you to understand others' reservations, and you seem to work creatively to help people get through their difficulties.

This makes you the 'energizer': among a group of independent thinkers, you are the ignition that sparks activity and change. You teach people under you well, through the influence of the **2**, and may choose teaching as a career, but you will expect dedication, quick thinking and excellence from your students. You may also be drawn to law through the **3** (defence, high-court public prosecutor or judge), or to self-employment – anything to avoid restriction. Any vocation that demands physical energy, quick wit and passion, or working as a wordsmith in any form, will be ideal. Fascinatingly, this has been the birthday of many politicians, actors, musicians and performers.

5 AT WORK

So, what kind of employee does your number make you? We've already seen that your birthday suggests you are much more comfortable working for yourself than for someone else, but when you're in a group how do you fit in? If you're the boss, are you a good one? Which fields are likely to be the best for your talents? And which the worst? And what about the male/female divide? Is a 5 female boss more desirable than a 5 male colleague?

Here, we get to grips with your career potential, your needs and 'must-have's for job satisfaction, and your loves and loathes work-wise, hopefully highlighting some areas where there is room for you to adjust your manner around others, to help you achieve what it is you're aiming for.

In the marketplace

Your number, as we have said, is perhaps the most 'exciting' of numerology, rather like the Fire sign of the zodiac, Leo. This means that, whether as corporation owner or floor-worker on the way up, you are aware always of the needs of the public at the centre of the world around you, with a heightened sense of your own desires and a driving feeling of duty to communicate and to invigorate others, and to create ideas and concepts for the preservation and progress of humanity.

MASTER OF MOTIVATION

Career-wise, the best word through which to understand your **5** id is 'determination'. Regardless of the field of expression you choose to work in, or the vocational opportunities thrust at you, your character seems to announce its fitness for motivating and directing where others must follow – and, at all times, that is towards *change*. Even if you work among equals in a low-profile atmosphere, when there is a crisis or a pressured situation that demands a swift response you will come naturally to the fore and calm those around you who are flailing, or you will reassure those who hesitate that *now* is the time to move on. **5**s frequently go into meltdown over the tedious frustrations of everyday living – train delays, traffic problems, when the telephone lines go down – but they are natural survivors in a serious crisis, and others look to you as a beacon in a storm.

In any work you do, your quick thinking and instinct for what may work will see you reach high levels of success (once you have mastered the art of completing the task at hand!), and this is why **5**s never stay below management level for long. Equally, the ability to turn situations around, and the freedom to operate spontaneously, is what forces so many **5**s into starting their own business.

WHERE DOES YOUR LIGHT REALLY SHINE?

Here are some of the qualities that **5**s bring to any job:

- A keen, questioning mind, resourcefulness and good communication skills mean you are likely to get ahead in any job, and especially likely to establish a successful business of your own if you desire it. Other people provide the necessary management and functionality, while you attract clients with your dynamic energy.
- You have acting ability, which means you can convince, seduce and sell any concept, gadget, product, invention or trend, or direct the public toward reforms. Your determination and need for adventure and variety will help you keep those around you awake, motivated and up-to-the-minute. You are your best business asset because it is difficult for people to refuse you on a person-to-person basis. You are, quite simply, irresistible!.
- You enjoy mental challenges, travel and adventure, and will thrive on a career that guarantees space, stimulation,

and an appreciation for your variety of talents. You certainly wish to be paid well for the work you do, but – overwhelmingly – you want to do something you love, and where you feel most useful. Payment is a bonus!

- The policy you live by – of never allowing life to become dull – pushes you to excel at what you do, and makes you naturally attracted to people, and to interesting work that has a varied menu from day to day. The minute a job becomes routine, you will leave it!
- You don't easily take orders from others – apart from when you can see that someone has the method and resources you require to succeed. This is you as the *opportunist*.

This makes you a person with unlimited skills and options. Where certain numbers have just one or two really clear lines of endeavour in which they will fly high, you can make a success of almost any course of work that allows you the kind of variety and freedom outlined above.

In any vocational path that demands that you develop new contacts, clients or projects, you are in your element. Careers that work well with this kind of talent include ...

Design: fashion/interior/graphic You have the flair and courage to break the rules, and you see what the market will want ahead of its time. Bold colours and new designs and fabrics are attractive to you, so you will experiment with them rather than continue beating a familiar path.

Property management and development Real estate interests you, and you love the freedom of ranging from place to place as part of your work day. You see what can be done with a site or in a location – and frequently redesign the 'flow', wanting open-plan, spacious interiors and uninterrupted outlook. Female **5**s especially will prosper in this field.

Publishing Communicating is the challenge, and you enjoy contributing as an illustrator, writer or promoter of new titles and types of work. Whatever area you are drawn to, you will find unconventional and exciting ways of doing things, and be known as progressive within your spectrum.

Government You're not the civil servant, but rather the boundary-rider! You love to challenge authority for the sake of forcing progress, and also love the spotlight, the chase, and questioning methods, old ways and prejudices.

Teaching and public speaking These careers demand entertaining speakers, and your active brain and memory, and colourful recollections, help you execute the demands of these jobs adroitly.

Health industry (especially sport, nutrition, fitness) The long hours are a killer for mere mortals, but a **5** will easily cope. The variety of work is a bonus, and activity and exercise will stimulate your senses for the better. Physical activity is perfect for you – or rather, *balanced* physical activity, because, as we learned earlier, a balanced attitude to all that you undertake, or are interested in, is paramount to your eventual success and well-being.

If your LIFE number (*see page 214*) is **7**, you will be likely to specialize, teach or do research; if it's **6**, or if the letters F, O or X are dominant in your name, you will be extremely good with patients and counselling the sick (a dietician, perhaps, or worker in a rehabilitation unit).

Art, literature, music These are areas that often entice the interests of a **5**. This is partly because they allow you freedom to work in your own space, in your own time, creating art, playing music, writing creatively, but also because you are drawn to the colour, energy, beauty and satisfaction of creating itself.

IT The computer world isn't boring for you, as you create new uses and applications for advancing communication and technology. You may be skilled at writing new programmes, or running a business from your computer, the flexible hours being ideal – not to forget the speed at which you can send your message through to others.

Drama, cinema, radio, TV You are at home in media-related jobs because of their potential for reaching large numbers of people. Where many are drawn to the buzz of this industry but worried by the lack of security or fear of going freelance, this registers as a 'plus' for a **5**. Directors, writers, actors, musicians – all find expression in this area, and enjoy the unusual pattern of work hours it entails. The weeks/months in rehearsal, and then on camera, followed by the 'holiday' season when you're waiting for the next 'big thing' to come along, again grants you the time for adventure and study, and to live an unconfined, unique life.

This list isn't exhaustive – a **5** can thrive in so many different career paths, as long as they offer freedom and the chance to work creatively – but it does offer a taste of what kind of fields suit your number.

And for luck?

Whatever your work, you will achieve your maximum potential if you use a name to work with that includes the letters E, N or W. Remember this when you are choosing a company name, if you go into business for yourself. It will help, too, for you to optimize your energy and positive attitude, if you decorate your work environment in the gentle colours of lilac, wisteria, lavender, pink, cerise and raspberry. If you are going for an important interview, these colours would make a positive choice in your outfit, as they help you to project yourself in your strongest light.

WORK PROFILE

The 5 female boss

Distinctively dressed, **physically fit** and making the most of her '**va-va-voom**', the **5** female in charge is an excitable, **vibrant** force. Exuding a fun yet **authoritative** energy across the office floor, she is recognized by her wit and need for results – yesterday. She juggles the landline with her cellphone and online conversations with her gal pals, a cloud of glorious perfume wafting in her wake. We all know exactly where she is – even on the move!

The men she works with give her **respect**, and may be not-so-secretly in lust with her. Her desk isn't tidy, for she is unwilling to waste time on anything deemed mundane, but signature touches announce to visitors that they are in her domain; her ultra-feminine colours (pink, lilac) are in evidence. **Colourful conversations** with clients and international peers are often held in their respective languages, and her **razor-sharp** appraisals are legendary. She is always off to the next appointment, or running out of town, and if she's late for a meeting she'll waltz into the boardroom **brimming with energy** for what must be achieved, firmly believing that her colleagues know she is late for a very good reason, never offering an apology. No one minds, for she **sets the scene** in her own unique way and gives one hundred and fifty per cent at the gathering. Woah!

Her strengths lie in **quick-mindedness**, creativity and **analysis**, and having a vision toward **progressive** trends, but she'll need **back-up**, reminders about the other more practical matters and someone to make her take time to eat healthily and exercise each day. The **5** female boss is a **hard act to follow:** all others will need to do is to keep up with her, anticipate her shortfall, take messages, make notes, fill her diary in, and be ready to move, change, travel and stay in touch, wherever she may be. Worth it, I'd say.

WORK PROFILE

The 5 male boss

Less of a peacock than his female counterpart, the **5** male boss is nevertheless clearly at the centre and **in the know**. Touches of his personality, once you know it, are evident from the front door to the top of the building. **Fun-loving**, **quick-witted**, clever and **multi-talented**, he is possibly multilingual, and quite the **entertainer**. He may disarm you with his daily jokes, and is extremely communicative *online*. His almost **frenzied juggling** of phone calls, e-mails and faxes may frustrate you completely – and you'll be expected to keep up! You'll have your work cut out, but it *could* be the most exciting time in your life.

Aware of his shortfalls, he'll be the first to arm himself with the necessary practical people, to cover all his bases. **Results-driven**, he wants to 'get there' and take others with him – and he believes in **rewarding** others for their initiative. He thrives on office interaction, encouraging social functions outside office hours, all of which he feels promotes the **goodwill** and solidarity necessary for success.

A **visionary** with the gambler's spirit, he will **take chances**, play with ideas, put unlikely people together and achieve a stimulating exchange for any new project. **People skills** are his strong suit: he has everyone's contact details and is able to reach, convince, charm or cajole any number of people to join him on projects – that's projects *plural*, for he has **many irons in the fire**. You might think him offhand, but it's probably just that he has grasped the facts and moved on. He loathes the mundane, so you had best come up with **exciting** presentations! His dress style is **distinctive**, but signs of his fun-loving flair are for a trained eye (quirky tie, odd socks) and not at the expense of a well-cut suit or an expensive shirt! This **jet-setter** must look **immaculate** wherever he finds himself.

WORK PROFILE

The 5 female employee

You noticed her the first day she arrived, with her gossipy conversation and her ever-changing wallpaper on her PC. But if you think she's flaky, think again. She has an ear on everything happening around the workplace, and she will soon know everyone's secrets, strengths and weaknesses. Not that she will break a confidence – she has a strong sense of needing to know just where any enemy camp may reside. Just expect a **5** employee, however, to **know exactly what's going on** around her, and to bide her time until such knowledge is a help to her in influencing her actions or facilitating her **need for progress**.

She is **flexible, competitive** and a veteran communicator, and she is not going to be working for someone else for too long. This is a girl **on the way up**, and she knows how to use her **considerable assets** to get there. You don't have to ask her to do anything twice, although she hates menial tasks, boring, stuffy people and a coop for an office. She is the girl who needs her space to be **open**: if she's confined she is likely to work out in the hall rather than sit facing the four walls. This isn't someone suited to limitation, drudgery or the mundane, and she'd do her all to change her position and circumstances if this was the case.

She has progressive ideas and brings an **eager, free-thinking spirit** into the work space, like opening a window of opportunity. Her energy and **agreeable nature**, and gracious, **curious** and **willing** personality, should have her moving toward a more suitable position soon. The more she is challenged and encouraged to develop her creativity, the greater her **confidence**, and although she doesn't sit still for long she will surprise her superiors with her **unique**, inventive and **enterprising** skills. This **5** female employee shows what **personal development** *really* means.

WORK PROFILE

The 5 male employee

Not one to get left behind by the female **5** in the other corner, he exudes **charm** and wit, **humour** and **flair**, and what he lacks in sophistication he makes up for in energy, a **willingness to learn** and ability to communicate. The **5** male at work in a subordinate job is biding his time, keeping his eyes and ears open, plugged into every opportunity to develop skills and **absorb knowledge**.

His dress lacks refinement but he is distinctive and generates sex appeal with a dash of **wit**. If his ideas are not heeded by his superiors, he will become **insecure** and frustrated, for he is an ideas man – happy enough being a team player for a while, as long as he feels appreciated for his **originality**. His desk is a mess because he is dwelling in the world of ideas, thinking to the future. A mentor will coach him in protocols, the completing of necessary tasks, listing priorities and adhering to office rules. He is funny and **good company**, but relationships don't run smoothly for him, as he likes variety and **freedom** to do what he pleases (female colleagues take heed!). He wants to get his career on track first, then ... there will always be something else. He is exciting, **unpredictable**, exuberant, **spirited**, daring, versatile and **sexy**, and not easily contained.

Ask him to do menial tasks at your peril, but throw your worst at him and be **amazed** at the way he handles tough assignments. He can stay up late or work into the night, and is ready to travel to sub-zero temperatures at an hour's notice, if it means he will get further up the ladder and out into the real world himself. Challenge him, trust his **creativity** and **enterprising capabilities**, but don't stifle him or get in his way. He has **places to go**, people to see, and he's in a hurry to consume the experience life offers – and, of course, he'd love to take us all with him.

Ideal world or cruel world?

Best and worst jobs ...

IN AN IDEAL WORLD

Best job for a 5 female: Head of performing arts programmes anywhere in the world, or arts programmer for a TV station (variety, creativity, recognition for achievement)

Best job for a 5 male: Travel co-ordinator for adventure-seekers/safari guide (varied, artistic, crazy hours, dangerous at times, envied by others, brings effortless sex appeal!)

IN A CRUEL WORLD

Worst job for a 5 female: Office manager of a recycling plant (responsibility, monotony, lack of creativity, low sense of personal status)

Worst job for a 5 male: Prison guard (regular hours, limited scope, little or no room for improvement of the human condition) or PA to an actress or famous author (always answerable to someone else, never being the star!)

5'S CHILDHOOD

Seeing the way a number expresses itself in someone very young is fascinating, for the tendencies and responses are all in their infancy – and yet plain to see. Some facets of a number's power need to be grown into, and take time to reveal how they will be dealt with by the developing character. Sometimes the strength of a number can be a frustration when we're young.

If looking back on your own childhood through the lens of your number, you should discover – with considerable humour and irony – a renewed understanding of some of the difficulties or excitements you experienced. Or, if you have a child who is also a **5**, you may learn something more useful; it is an advantage to understand the qualities a number exudes over an awakening personality, especially in relation to talents and career strengths, as it might save a lot of frustrations. You'll be able to appreciate the positive traits, and handle negative ones more sympathetically.

Here, we take a detailed look at what it's like to be a child bearing your number. But what about the other numbers? Perhaps you have a child who is a **7**, and you'd like to know what that means? Or maybe you'd like to gain insight into friends' and siblings' childhoods, to see if it sheds any light on the people they have become today? A short profile is given for each number, along with advice for a **5** parent on dealing with other-number offspring.

Just as your own parents would have discovered when you were a child, the hardest thing with a **5** child is getting them to sit quietly and listen, or follow any rules you lay down. **5**s, as you know, like to challenge old dictates, and experience or facilitate change for themselves. They are not always happy to do it your way ...

The young 5

A child born on the 5th, 14th or 23rd is very curious about the information they are given, right from the earliest age. A **5** child creates their own vocabulary, their own moral convictions, their own look, their own highly unusual manner and viewpoints. They often make us laugh with their grasp of a situation or their clever mimicry of family and friends. When a young **5** is dressed in a style similar to their siblings, they will find a way to alter the length of the coat, or hitch a dress up higher with a belt. They will wear anything with individuality, flair and a hint of sexiness – such teen queens!

The **5** child – at least until puberty – is strong and physically active, often sporty, energetic, quick to understand, and an inquisitive soul who wants to get on with things and not be held in check by others, however wise the parental eye might be. Does this mean they're restless and impatient? Yes! And this could bring frustrations and some confusion, in terms of their ability to communicate the inner drive they have to keep things moving forward, but a **5** child is always able to lighten their load with humour and spontaneous wit.

In childhood, a **5** needs careful handling. A bright mind bursting with excitement – with a disinclination towards restriction – needs subtle direction. They have a tendency to fritter their time away – disrupting classroom learning with clowning, influencing their friends to behave badly, and talking while teachers or elders are speaking – which leads to wasted opportunities for all. The young **5** needs discipline and focus; otherwise, life is going to be very disappointing for them. Naturally seeking variety and independence, they are on a quest to expand everything – and must be guided carefully, so that they learn to complete each task that they are given. This will require consistent

5's toys

Train • Aeroplane • Boat • Card games • Puzzles • Board games • Surfboard/skateboard • Roller-skates • Artist's brushes and paints • Kite • Tent and sleeping bag • Racing cars (for boys *and* girls) • Musical instruments

parental supervision and loving patience, and humour is the best companion on this journey. There is a noteworthy caution for all **5**s against over-indulgence or excessive eating, drinking, and the like; **5** children require lessons and guidance to develop personal discipline and a *balanced* attitude toward life's pleasures.

A **5** child's determination is a plus-point, but their boredom threshold will be an issue. Adults and teachers need to set them fresh challenges and allow them scope for exploration and adventure through a variety of interests and activities, in order to channel their enthusiasm.

A **5**'s greatest challenge through life (and it's a journey that begins at the cradle) is to *complete* anything – to stick at the task in hand, to study, to concentrate their effort on learning to develop those natural talents toward completion. If they only knew that, ironically, this is the 'key' to unlocking personal freedom! They are determined to travel the difficult path of the restless adventurer, and to help a **5** child to learn application and self-discipline is quite a task!

Help can be found in the form of 'quiet time': turning off the television, loud music and computer games. Ensure that there are some hours of complete quiet – a place for the **5** child to sit and relive their stimulating events, a table with clean paper on which to draw or write. Give them some simple puzzles, so that they can find completion out of what may seem chaotic. Paints and coloured pencils, musical instruments, storybooks, building blocks – all offer a way to demonstrate the process of creation. So, too, does cooking with your child, as **5**s love to cook, and for them to create something delicious is great fun and a perfect 'tool' that proves there is a beginning, middle and end, so that the outcome is successful. The lesson is that 'time' is involved, and that one must wait for the process to reach a successful completion before giving up and moving on to the next thing.

Just as in adulthood, **5**s suffer from being misunderstood: a **5** child often seems so restless in their private hours, and so demanding of having freedom, that they may not learn to express or harness their talents early on. Because their tendency is to flit from interest to interest, friend to friend, there is a danger that they may be thought 'scatterbrained', and they may consequently miss out on being included or chosen as a team members. Sports captain, school prefect or member of the debating team might be denied – despite their real suitability and talent. They are truly affectionate, compassionate and altruistic souls who crave to feel appreciated, useful and to share love. This **5** child should – with the wise guidance of parent, teacher, mentor or coach – grow into a fine contributing adult, and, like a fine wine, will improve with age.

There is an ultra-sensitive side to this **5** child, susceptible to others' moods and criticism, to food, sound and pollution. Their nervous system may give their parents cause for alarm, when they burn out from either physical extremes or nervous exhaustion. This might be called the 'phoenix effect' – the 'crash and burn' that we touched on earlier. So what can a parent do? Allow a complete crash, down and out – permission to be sick granted! Then the **5** can set about reconstructing the self. This won't happen too often, because **5**s really hate to be ill, as it's such an utter waste of their time. Just as they get on with most things, they take stock – not to mention any necessary medicines – and rebirth, just like the phoenix rising from the ashes.

A **5** child has, perhaps, almost too much to give, and too many directions to go in, or choices to make (even in adulthood). It's not easy to impress this child, and, as they are rather keen observers of the human condition, parents should be aware that they are under the microscope. If you're a **5**, you too were once like this! A **5** child needs, above all, consistency, and their parents must be loving guides who set reasonable boundaries for this adventurous, creative and expressive child.

The 1 child

This resourceful child has a different way of thinking, and will stand to one side and evaluate things without pressure. Repeat Grandma's sound advice on any subject to a **1** under the age of six, and they'll simply ask, 'Why?' Ignoring the social expectation to conform, **1** children often make us laugh with surprise.

A **1** child is tough and active – an inquisitive soul who wants to get on with things and not be held in check by others, however wise the parental eye might be. Stubborn and impatient, **1**s frequently suffer by questioning – though not from rudeness – the authority of a parent or teacher. **1**s break down tradition and find new ideas to form a fresh understanding of the world we're in. Your **1** child needs careful handling: a bright mind bursting with interest and disinclined to authority needs subtle direction. If **1** children dominate their friends and talk over their family it can make them socially inept and unable to co-operate in love relationships later in life, leading to loneliness rather than just self-reliance.

A **1**'s greatest challenge is to learn to live in a social world and understand that they are not inevitably right. To foster a **1**'s unique personality and avoid insensitivity to others, let them behave like an adult. This confidence a **1** child will ably repay. **1** children suffer from being misunderstood, as they're often so happy in their private hours and so demanding of having their own time that they may not learn to express their need for others. The seeds are sown early as to how to approach another person for signs of affection, so a canny **5** parent might simply wade across the private moat and cover their **1** child with kisses when the time seems to demand it. You share many similarities with your independent explorer-child, so don't be afraid to offer them some parameters: you'll both be happier for it.

The 2 child

All children born on the 2nd or 20th need affection and a peaceful environment to grow up in. Those born on the 11th or 29th are a little different, being master number **11**s with **2** as the denominator, and they have an old head on young shoulders from the beginning of their lives. But even they – for all their drive toward excitement and adventure – will be happiest if their home life is mostly secure and tranquil.

These highly sensitive and intuitive children know what you will say before you say it. They are also dreamy and process ideas in their sleep, waking to instinctive and wise solutions to their problems. But they are vulnerable, and need reassuring more than most numbers. They are acutely sensitive to criticism, feeling that all comments are proof that they're not quite good enough, so you need to deliver your words with tact and an awareness of their needs.

2 children are talented artists, actors, dancers and/or musicians: they know how others *feel*. A **2** child prefers to support friends and family as often as possible, and this can make them a doormat ready to be walked on unless those they live with are alert to their inclinations. If the **2** is an **11**, the wish to help out will be very strong indeed, but these children also have a finely tuned moral sense and will be offended by injustice – especially against them! Don't dish out judgement until you have all the facts.

2s are good healers and can make others feel better. Knowing when to cuddle or touch and when to be quiet, they often have a stillness which works miracles around the sick, the sad and the elderly. A **5** parent with a **2** child must be careful not to ignore their input or talk across them, nor be impatient with them – and must also not forget how much joy and support they receive from their gentle, intelligent **2**.

The 3 child

From the cradle, **3**s hold parties and like to mix with other children. They have a capacity to laugh and precipitate laughter, even when things go a little wrong. **3** children are like the reappearing sun after rain, and their energies can be restorative for everyone. Creative and playful, nothing keeps them low for long.

Like a juggler keeping plates and balls in the air, **3**s have several activities and talents on the go from the start. This can be a problem, however: making decisions is hard for them, and they need a wise older counsellor who can talk out the options and give them room to think. Even then, a decision once reached can always be changed – and a **3** child will find a way to run in several directions at one time.

Keep your **3** busy with lots of artistic activities, using colours and textures – right from babyhood – to open their eyes to what they can do. Even before the age of ten, a strong personal taste will begin to develop – and it may not be the same as their parents'. Using up their flow of energy on a multitude of tasks will be demanding on both parents, but the **3** child does give a great deal back in return.

3s are talkers and have a witty repartee, even when tiny: you'll be surprised at what you hear from them sometimes, and will wonder where it came from. Naturally gifted at PR, they will talk you around when you are set against one of their wishes, but you will need to direct them now and again or nothing will ever be finished! A **5** parent with a **3** child must allow them scope to try things differently, and not be upset if they are sometimes messy or chatter too much. Draw clear lines for them to follow, and they will always come up smiling. Give them the freedom that you demand yourself, and encourage them to speak honestly.

The 4 child

Surprisingly insecure and in need of praise, these children are reliable and hard-working and want to do well. They are their own worst critics at times, second only to number **7** children, and they glow when appreciated. They are happiest with family around them – even extended members – and often prefer holidays in familiar places. That said, they can be very quiet and self-sufficient when required, for they concentrate well.

These are organized children who won't cope well if their parents aren't as organized as they are! Never lose a school form or an item from their games kit on a crucial day, as this will cause them serious panic. They like to have material possessions around them because this bolsters their feeling of security, and will manage their pocket money well, content to do odd jobs and chores to gain this reward.

4s love the earth and buildings. They will treasure a patch of garden given them to tend, or a garden house they can extend or build outright. If they are born on the 22nd, rather than the 4th, 13th or 31st, they will truly have architectural talents, and may follow design as a career later. All **4** children, though, are handy at craft work and excellent at projects which require intelligence combined with method to get something done. They hate being late and don't admire tardiness in others, either.

As children, **4**s are loyal and dependable to family and friends, and are more patient than many numbers. They will make light of complex tasks, but need to be allowed to do things their own way. A **5** parent may consider their **4** child unimaginative or plodding; but they simply have a different approach to the duties of life. **4**s feel more responsible towards others, where **5**s are daring and unconventional. This leads to stubborn clashes. You could learn a thing or two from your **4** about process and good management!

The 6 child

Here's a young soul in need of a peaceful haven, just like a **2**, but a **6** will literally feel ill if there is dissension around them. Always wanting to beautify their surroundings and make pretty presents for Mum, these talented, sensitive children have many gifts for creative expression. They will also nurse the sick cat or anyone who needs gentle kindness, but are not always robust themselves, and should be sheltered from bad weather or aggressive viruses.

As children, **6**'s musical talents should emerge – and they often have beautiful speaking or singing voices. They are also the peacemakers of the family – natural creators of balance and harmony. Give them a free hand with their bedroom and their flower garden, and be ready to learn from them. Both boys and girls usually make good cooks when they are older, too, so time spent in the kitchen won't be wasted. Birthday presents that foster their good eye – a camera or set of art tools – will usually fit them well.

Despite being sensitive to others and quite intuitive, **6** as a child is a little shy and needs drawing out – especially if there has been much change in their young life, because **6** children need stability and like to remain a tiny bit traditional. They become very attached to their home. But if their family life is unconventional they will ultimately adjust, because they offer their family a lot of love, and like to be shown love in return. Even the boys have a feminine side, which in no way calls their gender into question.

Good at school and almost as well-organized as **4**s, this is a number which needs time to grow into itself; **6**s really are enormously talented. A **5** parent must be gentle and considerate with a **6**, who is not as daring or adventurous as they are. But when a **5** needs a friend to listen, support, encourage, back them up, they will often find unsuspected reservoirs of strength in this interesting child.

The 7 child

Even in primary school this is a child with a focused mind and a strongly developed critical sense. A **7** child is perceptive and, sometimes, disarmingly quiet. They will often prefer adult company, as their peers will probably seem too young and underdeveloped to them. Wise and difficult to know well, these are children with a serious cast to their intelligent minds.

The fact that a **7** child can sit quietly and contemplate things deeply should not imply that they are introverted: quite the opposite. A **7** will grow into a very good host as long as the company appeals, and they have a lovely sense of humour, apparent from their earliest years – even if it does sometimes find expression at others' expense. They will rarely be rude, but certainly have a good understanding of all that has been said – and what has not been.

Listen to their impressions of the people they deal with!

All **7**s as children have an inward reluctance to accept other people's ideas automatically – rather like **1**s – but there is a special propensity to independence in a child born on the 16th. This is the number of someone who finds it difficult asking for what they want – someone who often feels as though they haven't been consulted as to their own wishes. And all **7**s certainly have definite ideas about what to believe.

7 children should be told the truth on virtually all matters; they will know if they are being deceived, and will respect being treated as an adult in any case. A **5** parent will understand this, as they feel similarly about fostering early strengths. While the **7** is more reserved, the **5** will understand their need for space. The **5** parent will want to offer advice, but the **7** child needs to experience these things for themself. Be ready for a bond that is expansive, creative and yet explosive!

The 8 child

Here we have a young executive in the making. Even when they are still at school these children have a canny nose for what will make good business – and yet they are generous, hard-working and prepared to learn everything it will take to succeed in this life. Children born on the 8th, 17th and 26th like to have charge of their own finances, and to be given scope to do 'grown-up' activities – organizing their own parties and making arrangements for outings with their friends.

These children have strength and energy, but mentally are reflective and wise, too. They always see both sides to an argument – so parents who ask them to choose sides, beware! An **8** makes good judgements, and even before the age of ten they have a sense of what is fair and what is morally right.

As this number rules the octave, many **8** children are extremely musical and have a wonderful sense of rhythm. This last even assures they can be good at sport, as it takes innate timing to perfect many physical skills. **8**s also like philosophical ideas and relish being given 'big concepts' to chew over, especially concerning politics or religious ideas. **8**s are proud, and like to research things carefully – so as long as they are not bored, you will find an **8** child with their head in a book or on the internet, or watching programmes that educate and broaden their vistas.

Try to understand that an **8** is always striving for balance, and this will help you to be pragmatic if they are sometimes pulling in the opposite direction from you. **8**s are loyal to those they love, but a delicate sensibility makes them also look at the other side of a story, or fight for an underdog. As a **5**, you understand the urge to succeed and the need to learn, and you recognize your child's potential, and will respect the qualities and mind of your **8**.

The 9 child

Here is a person born for the theatre, or to travel the world and befriend everyone. **9**s have an expansive view of things, and don't like to be restricted. With a good head for both science and the arts, there are many career directions a **9** may take, so parents will have their work cut out trying to help them choose. However, because the number **9** is like a mirror, with every number added to it reducing again to that same number (for example: 5+9 = 14, and 1+4 = 5), **9** children are able to take on the feelings of just about anyone, which is why they are so artistic and good at drama and writing.

From their first years in school it will be clear a **9** child has a wonderful dry sense of humour and a taste for the unusual. **9** children are not often prejudiced and seem to be easy-going – though they are sensitive to the atmosphere around them, picking up vibes like a sponge. If you speak to them harshly they will take it seriously, and are protective of others who seem to be hurt in this way too.

9s have a delicate relationship with their parents, but particularly with the father figure. A **9** girl will want to idolize her dad, and will feel desperately disappointed if circumstances are against this, while a **9** boy may wish to emulate his father – and yet they often grow up without enough input from this important person, who is busy or away. A **9** child must be wise ahead of their time, and so this lesson is thrown at them in one guise or another.

The more serious **9** might find life in the fast lane with a **5** parent entirely too exhausting, and beg to go off to boarding school or summer camp! But you do share a passion for travel and adventure, colour and drama, and time also improves things, as your maturing, non-judgemental **9** begins to better understand your spontaneity and freedom-loving nature.

5 AT PLAY

We have discovered how your number expresses itself through your character in relation to your family and your general personality, what instinctive reactions go with your number in everyday situations, and how it might shape your career path and colour your childhood. But every day our DAY number also influences the way we respond to the social world around us. So, what can it say about our leisure hours? Is yours a number that even allows itself to relax? (Well, you probably already have some answers to this one!) What can your number reveal about the way you like to spend your time, or how you achieve pleasure outside of duty?

Over the next few pages we take a look at what makes you tick, as a **5**, when you are unwinding – and how **5**s prefer to fill their time, if given a choice. Let's see whether you're typical in this respect ... And who knows – if you haven't already tried all the activities and pastimes mentioned, maybe you'll get a few ideas about what to put on your list for next time!

The 5 woman at play

Conformist domestic gender roles and the demands of menial tasks are hardly your cup of tea, nor is anything that requires you to be housebound. As soon as you feel confined, you start planning an away-day! We know that you can be competitive, and that you enjoy sports and a variety of activities, and love the thrill of competing. These same qualities influence the way you spend your private time. Your leisure hours include your partner and demand a challenge, if they are truly to feel like a chance to unwind.

Although you're not always romantic in the conventional sense, when it comes to impromptu activities with your lover, five minutes' notice to pack is three more than you need. You'll be the one surfing the internet, trawling the travel agents or making that call to arrange a last-minute outing, whenever a friend or lover is bogged down.

Like **3**s, you bring the party to an inert situation, and stir up events to make something happen. You cause the change in someone's behaviour, start a new trend or mine a new vein of riches; and so it is in your private leisure time.

You probably prefer to escape the well-trodden tourist paths when you holiday, though you will make friends in every new place. Go to an eyrie in the mountains, for which no tourist guide has written the obligatory form guide; travel is your life-blood, and you love colourful places and people, so you will enjoy taking friends and lovers on any of your adventure trips. Life will be dull if you are only permitted to 'chill out' in a spa for days on end, or be stuck on a desert island – though your overcooked nerves would thank you for it occasionally. A long boat trip where you're confined with an uninteresting band of tourists would be torture. You will set off on a path no matter where it might lead, or whatever – or whomever – you may meet along the way. When you head for the country you, along with any **1** present, lead the walk and find an unexplored track. Companions will have to stretch to keep up with you.

Oceanic paradise holidays could be your thing, provided they offer a chance for you to get physical with your time (not just sexually!), allowing you to water-ski or sky-dive, instead of sitting listening to others' silly chat. Blue horizons stimulate your creative ideas, so staring at the skyline can be a prop for your imagination. If a friend recommends a venue, you'll be happy to start there and then add on an excursion to somewhere they've never heard of: a **5** woman repeats other people's behaviour only rarely, always looking for new places of interest, and attracts male admirers wherever she goes with her overnight bag.

Action breaks usually suit you well, and many **5**s set off in brightly coloured ski-wear or on spear-fishing expeditions – or on a ballooning holiday in the Andes – just to combine their physical drive and exploratory urges with a chance to think in boundary-free places.

Leisure weekends spent rearranging your home are a buzz – but not acting as the housekeeper. **5**s love to cook, but, having used several pans, need outside help getting everything back into order. You do need to recharge your energies and refresh your interests, so changing your environment regularly is one solution, as is moving house or redecorating. These options fall into the 'joy' zone. Many themes or styles excite your senses, and, as long as it is different and entertaining and adventurous, you are happy.

In the garden you'll demand the freedom to design the space, and leave the spade work to hired help in the guise of **4**s – not because you're unwilling to put the energy into doing it, but because the fun part for you is the creative planning. You're not at all concerned with the completing of the project, and will have moved on to (or into!) the bedroom, with a glass of champagne offered to the labourers, by the time the work is done. And you'll already be planning the party you can host from your new space.

The 5 man at play

You are just as much of a freedom/action addict as a **5** woman (are we surprised?), and your overnight bag has seen a lot of use. Travel is part of your weekly life, and your passport is never far from your side. This sets the tone for much of your hobby-time.

Being impatient in all you do, speed tends to creep into your leisure time, and you will be the smiling recipient of a gift experience spent at a car racing track, or skydiving from light aircraft. Your need for adventure dictates your taste, and you cram a lot of energy into a spare day, so early starts are usual for you. Anything unconventional and vigorous takes priority – and, if you can take along a lover who enjoys the same thing, that's fine! Physical pleasures are part of leisure time for **5** men, so 'naughty weekends' might become a regular feature.

A **5** man is an adrenaline demon. If anyone dares you to learn to fly a plane or spend a week at the bottom of the sea, you'll sign up for the task and bet on yourself to outdo others along the way. Going on a retreat to a monastery might prove more of a difficulty, given your natural and healthy libido, but you'll give it a go for the sake of a challenge. You may even come out well for it. Fresh activities have the capacity to feed your adventuring spirit and, let's face it: **5**s of both sexes are addicted to chemical rushes and hedonistic freewheeling. You love to perform for a crowd, explore new territory, and be physically daring for an amused audience. And don't they all just love to watch?!

Travel offers fresh places and new faces, but the need to change your environment regularly might persuade you to invest in a weekend cottage – perhaps by the sea, so you can sail or swim. When it comes to where you go, and how you get there, you are hard to predict. Most **5** men prefer jetting off to modern places and new concepts, rather than taking the slow boat to charming old historic towns – unless these quaint spots have been sympathetically brought into the modern era. The New World (east and west) may attract you – cities like New York and Beijing, or Sydney and Perth, which buzz and support your multi-faceted personality. Or you will love the shifting moods of places as old as Rome or Prague – choosing a different season each time, to get to know it. You pack your wild imagination in your luggage – along with the phrase book and good shoes. **5** men never arrive and expect the world to speak their language!

Physically strong, and never able to be entirely still, you have good skills for taking on DIY jobs and carrying them out with professional attention. Many a **5** man boasts the bruises and hammer-blows of a weekend spent installing a new work-shed or gym – or perhaps, on a more gentle level, new sound equipment or a home cinema.

Movies are a joy for you – travelling to another person's world. And anyway, the adventurer in your personality likes to demonstrate how it can play a number of character roles, and acting gives you a creative outlet and variety of personality types to play at. Each new role is an adventure.

Day-trips also suit your wanderlust, heading off into little-known areas and uncharted waters. Detours and side-trips are what others can expect when – and if – they are brave enough to travel with you. The social animal in you enjoys good food and spending time with stimulating friends, and will soon nose out a new pub or bar, or a stylish venue which hasn't yet been taken over by the trend-followers. Like **1**, you are a trend*setter*, and you possess the additional charm of loving to bring your favourite crowd with you, to treat them to your discoveries.

Did we say 'leisure time'? On reflection, there's nothing very leisurely about it!

5 IN LOVE

Love: it's what we all want to know about. What's your style as a lover? And your taste – where does that run? Do you want a partner who is, ideally, as emancipated as you? Or would you rather have a love in your life who is happy to give you freedom, and watch patiently while you make your own discoveries? Everything about you screams 'spontaneous non-conformist', but is this all there is to your love life?

Our first task is to consider how you see others as potential partners, and what you are likely to need from them. Why are you attracted to someone in the first place? This is where we begin ... But then you might like to pass the book across to your other half (if you have one), for the second subject of discussion is: why are *they* attracted to *you*? What does it mean to have a **5** lover?

Telltale traits of the 5 lover

- Creative, ardent, demonstrative, eager
- Fun-loving, exciting, imaginative, sensuous
- Communicates intentions across a crowded room
- Loathes borders and boundaries: 'Don't fence me in!'
- Loves surprises
- Dresses uniquely, with dash and wit
- At times, ventures where angels fear to tread

How do you do?
A **5** IN ATTRACTION

That fascinating person who looks like a breath of fresh air – who stands out as poised and enigmatic, but also sexy and loads of fun – is the one among the crowd of people listening to your jokes whom *you* want to know better. Your ideal love will be someone whose face shines, and whose mouth is expressive and full of soft laughter. They will be enthusiastic about whatever is happening but also mysteriously self-contained; in their present environment, they are alive to the occasion. A **5**'s desirable date has a good mind and considerable aesthetic charms. You are never drawn to anyone – whatever their other claims – who is either safe or predictable: the challenge, the hunt, is part of the intoxification of love!

Demanding a challenge like this, you inevitably end up

chasing someone who's not only hard to get but also (quite possibly) already spoken for. If you are gently denied first time round, this will make you try afresh with a new strategy. Sexy and dynamic, you never give up or call it quits. Many **5**s acquire lovers with complicated pasts – and who can you blame for this but your own seductive, tangled self! And who can deny you, either? With that humour and those smouldering eyes, **5**s exude an informal charm and *physical* self-confidence that is devastatingly attractive – though this may, in fact, mask the insecurities that lurk beneath the surface of the independent, freedom-loving persona you seem to embody.

The secret of your success

Your command of languages and your individuality assures that you have an excellent success rate with the opposite sex. You set up magical and unusual dates, and a weekend away with a brand-new lover helps both parties to leave any inhibitions behind. But sometimes you do come on very strong – for, when your heart (or sex drive) is engaged, you are a force to be reckoned with. This may be more than the faint-hearted can endure: a new love may not be willing to move as fast as you do. If you don't wish to frighten your date out of their wits, and dash your hopes of showing them what you're really made of, try to remember to pedal gently for a day or two! This will allow time for you to weave your magic spell a little, before you entirely take their breath away.

No one can ever guess what might be on your mind, or where a romantic dinner for two make take them, with you in the driving seat. Sunset on a ferry boat or sunrise at a mountain-top café, a picnic on the riverbank or breakfast in a foreign city – all are equally possible. You have a knack for staying one step ahead of your bemused companion, and this will remain true even should you make it to your golden wedding anniversary, if you are genuinely in love (although it's quite an achievement for change-loving **5** to find a companion who can hold them for fifty years!).

Go easy!

Smooth with words, and having an appreciation for the unexpected, you know exactly when to let actions take over from flirtation – but be careful you don't find you've attracted more admirers than you'd bargained for! To the one who watches you strutting your stuff in front of the crowd, you are charismatic, entertaining and a vigorous suitor – which would be counted by anyone you've attracted as potentially serious interest. But you're not always sure about making a commitment, so if you're just getting close to a person, and haven't yet decided where it might lead, be careful not to give off confusing signals.

Remember: you are the consummate salesperson, and you may get too caught up in selling yourself, or just in the all-important excitement of the challenge factor, so please be thoughtful towards your quarry, as well as kind and (invariably) charming. **5**s are the worst heartbreakers, and you don't always consider the impact you're having! Try to respect your admirer's potentially wounded feelings.

Speaking of which ... You can never love someone who doesn't command your respect, or allow you absolute freedom to be – and do – whatever, whenever. So, if that gives any mortal being hope that they can fulfil all the qualities of tolerance and lack of possessiveness that they would need in order to make you happy, perhaps it's time to let them read over your shoulder, so they can see what they've let themselves in for, in loving a **5** ...

To have and to hold?

LOVING A NUMBER 5

If you love someone who is born under this charismatic and adventurous number, they will stretch your sense of self-confidence (not to mention patience!) and demand that you acquire great intuitive skills as well, to understand the difference between what they *really* want and what they may *say* they want. **5**s never advertise their need for approval and affection from those closest to them, emitting an aura of self-reliance and cockiness; they often give the confusing impression that they are totally restless and unprepared for commitment, when they do, of course, need to be loved by a patient soul who doesn't hold on too tightly.

Though 'commitment-phobic' is partly true, no **5** is the total scallywag they seem! This means you need to see beyond the wrapping, understanding that there is, in fact, a very restless child inside every number **5**, male or female, and that this person needs lots of unrestrictive tenderness, alongside gentle signs of encouragement, from you. A **5** is something of a child in love, but don't be put off by this.

You've undoubtedly been attracted to a very exhilarating and perhaps gregarious soul. Your **5** love is surprisingly demonstrative – someone who captivates a crowd. If you're honest, that charming, sensuous, sexy personality is part of what pulls you: you must yourself feel drawn to people who are sparkling individuals, and you certainly like a challenge in love relationships, anyway – otherwise you'd never have got yourself into a love affair with a **5**.

Share and share alike

This risk-taking person will never let you settle into a routine or get caught in a rut. You are sure to be enjoying an unusual courtship, even after several years, forever doing things others would be too shy to try. You'll enjoy the physical aspects of your private time together, when it's just the two of you – though, with a number **5** you are likely to have to adjust to expanding your friendships and outings or holidays to accommodate best mates. And you will have to like or admire your loved one's friends, because they are the life's blood for a **5**, so it's best that you learn to adjust quickly. Book travel arrangements, but expect them to change, so that you can meet up with so and so, here or there.

You will learn to be flexible and – if this relationship graduates to a lifetime commitment – hospitable, too. The honeymoon may be interesting, to say the least, as you can expect to find that you are sharing your special time with new spouse's dear friends. But then, your **5** lover has a magnetic hold over you *and* your many friends, so understand that privacy can be hard to come by.

Expect the unexpected

Why are you so attracted, then? **5** has so many creative – and different – perspectives to offer you on life, and loves to keep moving. Nothing will be allowed to become humdrum – no dust ever to settle. This goes beyond the promise of an interesting sensual life together. You will see the world, learn dozens of words in several languages, live with a rollercoaster of feast followed by famine, and back to feast again. In short, surprise is the theme. Plus, how stylishly does your **5** turn themselves out? Their wardrobe is replete with fashionable clothes (budget permitting) and any garments that are striking and individualistic, downright sexy, colourful and sparkling, with inventive accessories. Don't chide them about the expense, because one of the things you probably love is that your **5** never dresses the same way as other people.

Socially, and at play, they take centre-stage in most

situations (even when you don't always want them to), and their personal image is crucial to what they do. Be sensitive to this when you are forming a critical statement: couch your words tremendously carefully, for **5**s are sensitive to criticism and take it *very* personally.

Are you discovering a somewhat dangerous aspect of your attraction – a restless and flirtatious spirit? This is certainly true: your **5** love is both emancipated and impulsive. This means that choices – which restaurant or holiday venue, where to park, which house to buy – are always varied, and drive their happiness. **5**s know what they want when they see it, and will seize the moment – relegating issues of common sense, affordability or sentiment to the rear! Even so, it grates when you feel your partner has a strong opinion about *everything*, and forgets to acknowledge the part you play – or worse, if you're not quite sure you're secure in this partnership. Your **5** is so out there in the whirl of life, people-orientated, emotionally changeable, so popular with the opposite sex, that admirers tend to gravitate to them rather like the proverbial bees to the honeypot; and, their dislike of restraint of any kind can make you feel insecure and uncertain of where the relationship is going.

Up to the challenge?

This natural free spirit, this true *character* with so much energy and charisma, attractive to so many, is not for a shrinking violet. Find tactful ways of voicing your needs, kill the (natural) urge towards jealousy, be interesting and adventuresome, and try to diffuse tense situations with humour. Confronting a **5** head-on will be explosive and unproductive.

If your **5** seems fragmented, uncommitted or uncaring, don't expect that this is going to change. But if you can enjoy the sometimes daring path of constantly wondering what to expect next, you'll be rewarded with a lover who exudes sexual magnetism, *joie de vivre*, and a child's enthusiasm for progress and adventure. You'll be much envied by most of your friends, and something unexpected will happen all the time.

The best thing is to be the person you were born to be. Don't wait for any **5** to make their mind up. Keep yourself invigorated, stimulated and interested, have your own friends, make plans and book outings, discuss your dreams – and invite your **5** to join in gently. Entice, seduce and excite them with the many possibilities on offer, and you will be well on your way to managing your **5** lover.

5 in love

Turn-ons:

♥ ✔ An ultra-sexy partner who is responsive and fun

♥ ✔ Someone who likes adventure, sporting activities and eating at exciting restaurants

♥ ✔ A person with a sense of humour and a warm laugh

♥ ✔ A creative, expansive, intelligent enthusiast who shares your determination to constantly move towards progress

Turn-offs:

♥ ✗ A clingy partner who asks too many questions or slows you down

♥ ✗ Someone who is dull or too practical about your dreams

♥ ✗ A lover who must have routine: you hate predictable plodders!

♥ ✗ Anyone who disapproves of you in front of others, or who tells you the ending of a movie before you get to it

5'S COMPATIBILITY

In this weighty section you have the tools to find out how well you click with all the other numbers in matters of the heart, but also when you have to work or play together too. Each category opens with a star-ratings chart, showing you – at a glance – whether you're going to encounter plain sailing or stormy waters in any given relationship. First up is love: if your number matches up especially well with the person you're with, you will appreciate why certain facets of your bond just seem to slot together easily.

But, of course, we're not always attracted to the people who make the easiest relationships for us, and if you find that the one you love rates only one or two stars, don't give in! Challenges are often the 'meat' of a love affair – and all difficulties are somewhat soothed if you both share a birthday number in common, even if that number is derived from the *total* of the birth date rather than the actual **DAY** number. In other words, if your partner's **LIFE** number is the same as your **DAY** number, you will feel a pull towards each other which is very strong, even if the **DAY** numbers taken together have some wrinkles in their match-up. You will read more about this in the pages that follow the star chart.

The charts also include the master numbers **11** and **22**: these bring an extra dimension to relationships for those whose birth-number calculations feature either of these numbers at any stage. (For example, someone with a **DAY** number of **2** may be born on the 29th: 2+9 = **11**, and 1+1 = **2**. This means you should read the compatibility pairings for your number with both a **2** and an **11**.)

Sometimes the tensions that come to the surface in

love relationships are excellent for business relationships instead: the competitiveness that can undermine personal ties can accelerate effectiveness in working situations. We'll take a look at how other numbers match up with yours in vocational situations. And, when it comes to friends, you'll see why not all of your friendships are necessarily a smooth ride ...

In all matters – whether love, work or friendship – you will probably discover that the best partnerships you make involve an overlap of at least one number that you share in common. A number **5** attracts other number **5**s in various close ties throughout life.

NOTE: To satisfy your curiosity, **ALL** numbers are included in the star charts, so that you can check the compatibility ratings between your friends, co-workers and loved ones – and see why some relationships may be more turbulent than others!

Love

YOUR LOVE COMPATIBILITY CHART

	1	2	3	4	5
With a 1	★★★★	★★★★★	★★	★★★	★★★★★
With a 2	★★★★★	★★★★	★★★	★★★★★	★
With a 3	★★	★★★	★★★★★	★★	★★★★
With a 4	★★★	★★★★★	★★	★★★★	★★
With a 5	★★★★★	★	★★★★	★★	★★★
With a 6	★★★	★★★★	★★★★	★★★	★★
With a 7	★★★★★	★★	★★★	★★★★★	★★★
With an 8	★★★★	★★★★	★★★★★	★★★	★★★
With a 9	★★★	★★★	★★★★★	★★	★★★
With an 11	★★★★	★★★★	★★	★★★★★	★★
With a 22	★★★★	★★★★★	★★★	★★★★	★★★★

6	7	8	9	11	22
★★★	★★★★★	★★★★	★★★	★★★★	★★★★
★★★★	★★	★★★★	★★★	★★★★	★★★★★
★★★★	★★★	★★★★★	★★★★★	★★	★★★
★★★	★★★★★	★★★	★★	★★★★★	★★★★
★★	★★★	★★★	★★★	★★	★★★★
★★★★★	★	★★★	★★★★★	★★★★	★★★★
★	★★★	★★★★	★★★	★★★★	★★★★★
★★★	★★★★	★★★	★★	★★★★★	★★★★
★★★★★	★★★	★★	★★★	★★★★	★★★
★★★★	★★★★	★★★★★	★★★★	★★	★★★★★
★★★★	★★★★★	★★★★	★★★	★★★★★	★★

5 in love with a 1 ★★★★★

Fizz! Bang! This relationship pops and crackles. You are extremely drawn to each other physically, and have a need to get out and feel the wind in your faces and the world around you under your feet. There is a strong magnetism between you, which is tangible to all those who see you together. You are not going to sit on your hands, either of you, and this relationship should be able to withstand most problems it encounters, for you work well with each other in almost all areas.

5 is as interesting and original as **1**: together, you are always up for a last-minute dash to some odd place to watch the sun rise. In fact, *you* can't sit in one place for long, and this is one of the few threats to your mutual happiness – because your **1** likes (and needs) solitude at times. How can **1** draft their new visions if you won't stay still long enough to let them get settled? You will need to work out how to give each other appropriate personal time.

Money will materialize well between you, for both of you have a capacity to think up ideas and work hard to make them realities. You easily promote your **1**'s skills and strengths, and know how to attract finance for your joint projects. Difficulty comes when you also want to spend a lot of money: **1** may not share this constant love of luxury. However, if the **1** can indulge you sometimes, it may not have to burgeon out of control! And you both like many nice things, so you just need to agree a limit.

What you will really enjoy together is a sexy love style which bends the rules that others seem to need to live by. You both enjoy the physical aspects of your relationship, and things may get very experimental. Suffice to say you are less likely to run out of steam in the bedroom than many relationships! This also means that you may never need – or want – to stray from one another, for you will never settle for the same old thing, or get stuck in a rut. You are both unconventional – the **1** almost as much so as you – and you will discover some very romantic, as well as sensual, ways to satisfy each other's curiosity.

You share a respect for education, and it is quite possible that you have several academic interests in common, and that you'll go on learning together for many years. You each have an intelligent mind and a good wit, so stretching yourselves together is a way to continually interest one another and keep things fresh. But you are given to ups and downs, or feeling the blues, so your **1** will have to be a wise counsellor, as well as a good lover. You are restless, and sometimes this footloose and fancy-free yearning can be more than either of you bargained for. Moreover, your standards are sometimes at odds, so, over the years, you will need to maintain your feeling of originality, and not slip into conventionalism, if your trust of each other is to stay strong.

You will need to unwind, and your **1** should help you if they can; you also need to offer the **1** tranquillity, and force some calm on them even when they seem to resist your electricity!

Key themes

5 loves freedom but **1** recreates a feeling of freshness and individuality daily • Both partners take chances and have a strong sense of daring • A very sexy relationship where each learns how to satisfy the other • Likelihood of earning well together and living with money

5 in love with a 2 ★

An interesting one, this, for there are some strangely unexpected similarities between these numbers – although, in the main, they couldn't be more different. It could perhaps be described as 'make or break'. **2** will chafe against **5**'s chattering and restlessness, never seeming to head to any place or find any peace inside, while **5** despairs of **2** hiding their light under a bushel. And, where **5** is the pirate adventurer, **2** is the yoga student; as **5** takes on a clutch of racy ideas and opportunities, **2** is busy shaking its head, wondering whether anything will come of any of it (unless the LIFE numbers suggest different strengths; *see page 214*).

But if the **2** willingly takes a back seat, and just tries to trust your instincts (which are very much those of the gambler!), it could be an interesting ride. **2** could certainly stage-manage your brilliant performances in business and, socially, make something extraordinary of you, and you will probably look to the **2** to make you feel more secure and organized. **5** is brilliant – there is no doubt – but will it wear on the **2** over time? These numbers are not natural friends, the one requiring gentleness and the other fireworks. And where **5** is so physical, **2** is so cerebral.

The similarities are not, at first, strikingly obvious, but on better acquaintance it will be clear that there is ground to build on between you. **5** and **2** are both people numbers, and there is a chance that you can widen **2**'s horizons, while they bring a more discerning group of people into the home, with whom you can develop stronger ideas. You need to be given projects, to ask for a direction to indulge in. You're not really practical, but tireless and full of energy. It's just that sometimes **2** wants to be quiet and think!

And, to be fair, **2**s do sometimes snuff out **5**'s wonderful enthusiasm for life and zany brilliance. Yours is a number that needs an audience, coming alive in situations that require daring. This is not to everyone's taste, but if **2** can lend you some strength and reassurance, it may be a relationship where miracles happen all around you both; and you may – as a team – affect the lives of many other people. Give a **5** a platform or a theatre in which to speak, and change the ordinary dullness that can be life every day. This is when **2**'s idealism cuts in, and they may think the world of their clever, inspiring **5**.

This partnership in love definitely works best if the **2** is very well-educated and philosophical, for then the **5**'s electric mind will be held by the breadth and dimension of **2**'s thinking. A **2** can help you to realize and actualize your ideas – concepts which will be songs in the wind unless a clever, reliable soul can plan a strategy to make use of them. You are a troubadour at times, and can be a wasted talent, and **2** is a dreamer, who may also let their best ideas evaporate. One of you has to get behind the other, and put smaller frictions aside to prioritize what is good. You can either widen each other's horizons, or tear away each other's gifts cruelly. **2** is more tactful, so if they really care for their fascinating **5** they will hold their tongue and try to make it a challenge to achieve the harmony they crave. It will be interesting, as I said in the beginning!

Key themes

Loving and ultra-sensitive **2** must learn to forgive much that **5** overlooks or deems unimportant • **5** desires freedom and their own time and space, but living with **2** can bring them more emotional security, order and refinement

5 in love with a 3 ★★★★

There are many overlapping qualities between these numbers, which share a love of life and a zany sense of humour. **5** can't help being attracted to **3** for their brilliance and energy. Each is a variant of the other – different shapes cut from the same cloth, perhaps. **5** excites **3**'s vivid imagination, and both of you enter into word-play and behavioural chess games which indicate to others the degree of tangible sexual attraction.

You have notched up a little more experience than the **3** in many respects, so what attracts each of you to the other is the opportunity to broaden each other's world. **5** loves to show eager and witty **3** how to shine in foreign places; and **3** makes **5** feel young and sexy all the time. You have a way of seeing the world – **5** in a funny but cynical manner, and **3** in a pithy but normalizing way. Neither of you waits for a better opportunity to come if a door opens and a chance arises to be spontaneous. 'Pack your bags,' you might tell each other, or, 'Try it now!' Neither of you needs a second invitation to anything much!

3 is naturally very sexy and attractive in the eyes of a **5**: **3** is perhaps the only number to be as comfortable with their sexuality as you! You are drawn to their charm, style and colour – for **5**s never lead a dull life. Physical compatibility is more than just a bonus if it happens: for you, it is an essential ingredient in a good relationship. **3** won't argue with this, and the sensuous side of your relationship together will play an anchoring role in keeping you interested in one another. But is there more than sex?

Certainly! Two numbers who speak well, think fast, love to dip their toes in the water of life are bound to get on. You are both tolerant of almost anything and anyone, which is something that can make or break many other relationships. If you are broad-minded and generous to others mutually, it makes for a better starting point. Also important is the fact that you like to get on with things, just as a **3** does. It doesn't take you days to act on an idea, nor does it take the **3** more than a moment to try something if it feels right. **3**s love water, and **5**s mountains – so you will meet each other for spontaneously planned rendezvous in both landscapes. You love oriental food and bubbly champagne, and **3** loves almost all good food and champagne – no conflict there. You're an outdoors person who dons the right attitude when the sun comes out; **3** always loves the sunshine and has a permanently tolerant view of a hot day. Bliss!

The relationship works best when both of your fine minds have been well-educated, which offsets a tendency to run at tangents just for the sake of excitement. Neither of you is necessarily deeply philosophical, but your electric mind is more inspired by **3**'s imaginative gifts and sense of optimism. **3** comes up with such innovations, and you know how to take them to the marketplace. This might strictly be business, but as you are uplifted by mental endeavour it can be very important in a daily routine that you respect, admire and promote each other's work lives. **5** is a hippy, perhaps, or a poet sometimes, but can often be a wasted talent; and **3**'s clever ideas also evaporate if there is no one to encourage and shape them. Oddly enough, you do this for each other.

Key themes

Both love freedom, which could create tense moments • Both have a strong sense of daring – especially sexually • Both prepared to find out how to satisfy the other • Shared humour a real feature of the attraction

5 in love with a 4 ★★

There are few areas of meeting ground between a **5** and a **4**, and it would be an extraordinary testimony to **4**'s determination if they are able to make this work! **5** buzzes and flies through a day, sometimes surprising themselves at how things manage to turn out so brilliantly, whereas the **4** will take care to see things through sensibly. This basic style carries into a romance, and you may drive each other to distraction in your opposing ways of tackling life.

Perhaps the initial interest can be explained by 'opposites attract'. A **4** will be mesmerized by your vitality and energy, and quick verbal ripostes. And you will be astonished by **4**'s groundedness and good sense – the way they can see through a tangled situation and make plain sailing of it. This amounts to mutual admiration. In terms of sexual tension, that, too, may come in this pairing. The **4** seems so fascinating, with their feet on the ground and their lack of interest in transitory passions; their very appearance of certainty is something for you to think about. And you will make the deep-thinking **4** wonder what is at the centre of all that energy. Plus you're sexy – let's face it! **5** is one of the sexiest souls in the number chart. But after the initial fizz and pop has gone a little flat, what happens next? You two are just so different.

A **4** will always be trying to hold a **5** still long enough to discuss the future, but **5** is living for the moment, expressing a different philosophy. 'Why worry about what may never happen?', you think; and this is anathema for wary **4**, whose sense of personal security cannot bypass a love relationship. Your flamboyance may needle **4** into the worst shows of anger and stubbornness; and **4**'s inflexibility in so many areas will almost certainly provoke real flashes of temper from you – patience is never one of your strong points. Your wit may be lost on **4** over time –

though initially it has such a striking appeal; and **4**'s way of asking so many questions, and taking little on faith, is not the way you like to do things.

No doubt you are charming and vivid, brightening the world for a sometimes overly burdened **4**. You may be the very splash of colour that takes away the dullness often demanded of **4**. And isn't it wonderful when a calm **4** can see a way across the volcanic ground left in your wake – keeping both of you cool together? Yet, while these truths are certain, the irritations may begin to pile up too high ...

5 speaks – and wants the world to hear – their inspirations; **4** would like a quiet place to think and get through the long list of tasks to complete before they can relax. **5** wants somewhere new and exciting to take a holiday – or, perhaps, to interrupt a boring day with a romantic lunch at the very least, or even a quick lunch hour spent in an extravagant hotel. A **4** will indulge this once or twice, but such flights of fancy on a regular basis will seem shallow and unfulfilling in the long term: and who's to say that's wrong? If **5** wants a last-minute trip to a Greek island, **4** will panic about the rush; and if **4** wants to head for the cottage in the country, **5** will miss the action in the city. If **5**'s middle name is 'spontaneity', **4**'s is 'planning', and the two, ultimately, are on a collision course. To work, this relationship will take as much flexibility as you can find, and as much indulgence as **4** can muster. And then, only *maybe*.

Key themes

5 loves freedom and **4** is left gasping • **4** wants to tie **5** down to fixed plans • Sexual attraction a plus, but may be short-lived • **4** is the planner, **5** the accident waiting to happen!

5 in love with a 5 ★★★

Well, now – this is sexual attraction on four legs! Your **5** is interesting, original, freedom-loving, just as you are, and always up for doing things at the last minute – rushing off to some strange place or other to watch the sun set, booking travel to exciting places, eating at trendy bistros with convivial groups of people ... You love the dynamism, the chance that things will be heaven or hell, the idea that anything goes. Here is a fierce pair of wills that match each other. But as you *both* know, **5** can't sit in one place for long, and this is one of the few threats to your mutual happiness. You will both be off whirling and twirling, taking centre-stage goodness knows where. How are you ever going to settle down to a true commitment or share time towards cementing this union, never mind growing within it?

You will need to work out how to give each other appropriate personal time *and* the necessary freedoms. Money will manifest well between you, *if* you work in tandem or in different areas within promotional industries (more about this in the work compatibility section; *see page 190*). But as a couple, you are likely to live the high life and take risks together.

Difficulty comes when both of you want to spend a lot of money, and you may not possess any sense of restraint or duty where saving is concerned. It is true for each of you that no sooner does money hit your hand than it flies out again, and sometimes this propensity to fritter your money away is totally out of control. Add to this the fact that the two of you are mutually culpable, and things could get very shaky. You both like many nice things, so you just need to agree on a limit and adhere to a budget.

Your sexy love style is a definite bonus, which is more than likely what attracted you to one another in the first place. Just as sensual, affectionate and physical as each other, you share that sense of adventure and dynamic energy that defeats most people. Unconventional in your approach to most things, you have a tendency towards over-indulgence in sensual pleasures, and you may also, perhaps, lack a sense of proportion, as far as your mutual need for variety, change and excitement is concerned. Sometimes you may even drive each other to craziness – public performances, or exhibiting a lack of restraint. Still, maybe it's fine if you both want it!

Two **5**s are hardly likely to bore each other in the bedroom, and have more shared energy than most relationships. However, because you are both such pleasure-seekers, desirous of variety, stimulation and the excitement that your passions inspire, you may stray from each other both easily and often, being unfaithful and breaking trust. This slides quickly – and predictably – into all the negative manifestations of insecurity, loss of trust and devastating disappointment where you both crash and burn. And this is why this partnership rates only three stars – but, in reality, your relationship may have more to say for it than that. It all depends on your (mutual) levels of maturity!

Key themes

Rejoice in each other's spontaneity, love of adventure and variety, magnetism, and personal creativity • Both attractive to the opposite sex • Share in quick mental responses, rapid analysis and desire for fun • Relationship of sparks, tempers and great activity • Jealousy can be a problem

5 in love with a 6 ★★

Opposites attract, and that can be a good thing – especially in this partnership, if you are willing to learn from the particular differences that each of you exhibit. **5**s are freewheeling, unconventional lovers, ardent, sensuous and quite demanding, where loving is concerned. Without disturbing **6**'s sensibilities here, your **6** bears the number of love, appreciation, nurture and friendship, and as such may find you entirely too rambunctious, once the initial phase of fascination and intrigue wears off.

If anything, it's you, the **5**, who should make every effort to get to know your **6** lover well, because if you do you will find that you share creativity, a love of the arts, and a fondness for the finer things in life – good food, creature comforts, firm friends and acquaintances. The **6** has the ability to add finesse to your appreciation, and fine-tune your skills. You will value your **6**'s excellent taste, easy good humour and manner, superb culinary skills – and you will learn from all of it. A **6** can get you to look at the world in a different light, and they may also just about persuade you to be more considerate and balanced in giving and receiving love and affection.

This is, of course, at best, because a **6** is a soul wanting to be loved above all else. They will force you to feel your emotions, ask you for a kiss, and tell you when you are being impossible – ever so gently.

If you are indiscriminate, self-indulgent or capricious, your **6** will pine and fret. **6**'s pain and hurt is related to needing love, whereas your own wishes are to be free to do as you please with whom you so desire. **6** is not spineless, but is made strong by love. Try to be as sincere, sharing and expressive as possible, if you care for this tender-hearted person and want to make the relationship work over time. And what the **6** will love about you is the way in which you sparkle (both for them and for others), your humour and daring, your complete disrespect for inherited ideas and institutions. This is not at all like **6**, but they are in awe of you for being a rule-breaker, and, if you don't abuse this power to speak out, you can be very exciting for a **6**, and open their horizons.

But most of the adjustments must come from them – is this too much to ask? – and it will be imperative that you curb the natural impulse to be impatient, unaccountable, unreliable and unrestrained just because your **6** wants assurances of love and devotion, or seems to take longer than you do to decide on a direction to take. You may then fall from grace in your **6**'s eyes, and so high are the ideals your **6** is looking for in others that it is sometimes unrealistic to expect anyone – especially a **5** – to live up to such a standard. However, you may not be the best person to help them realize they are after the impossible ...

Key themes

5 excites **6**'s pride in them • **5**s must expect invasions of privacy from friends, old school mates and overseas visitors • Magnetic sexual and creative field between you, but risk of areas of misunderstanding that cause insecurities and loss of respect

5 in love with a 7 ★★★

As with the previous pairing, opposites attract! Or is this really more about the challenge factor? Here, we have the naturally exuberant, freedom-loving, sexually demanding and adventurous **5**, fascinated and in love with the high-minded, intelligent, ever-challenging yet reserved **7**. The **5**, on one hand, is physical, materialistic, progressive, with keen intelligence and a quick grasp of most things, while the **7** is spiritual, analytical, cerebral, contemplative and a seeker of wisdom and truth.

There is no doubt that this relationship will stimulate you both for entirely different reasons, bursting with creative and inspirational discussions, evenings out, tête-à-têtes when your **7** can have you to themselves, or, at the end of a dinner party, when you find yourselves alone and in front of a crackling fire. I doubt that you were at the party the night before, though, because **7** doesn't favour those packed venues or mindless banter. This is a marriage of truly curious and inquisitive minds, in a way. Your **7**'s enigmatic reserve and intelligence are a magnet for you, and you seem to reach into your most spiritual inclinations when you come together with this number, because your **7** is capable of such depth, and you are – while bright and vivacious – more of a rocket on the way to Mars.

7 is a very private number, and things will teeter if you are in any way indiscriminate. Also, if you are too demanding (sexually or in your desire for answers about their life), you will lose them: **7**s insist on keeping some corners of their personality away from everybody else – even from you, and even if you are the love of their life. This will be a challenge every day – and in most situations where your affable and curious personality bounces in where angels fear to tread. Although **5**s are warm, unprejudiced and skilful in finding things out, even you may feel that there is a darker truth behind your **7**'s surface – experiences or loneliness that might explain their complexity and enigmatic depth. You may never be allowed to go there. Don't attempt to blast your way through this reserve, but try to allow your love time. **7**s will say whatever they are going to say to their own agenda – and pushing will alienate you both.

You are an extroverted introvert, while your **7** is a little bit introverted – at least in some departments. Family memories and early shaping experiences cast a long shadow. A **7** lover needs you to be aware of their need for truth and honesty, but also their desire for independence. Some of these ideas seem contradictory – yet they are all true. If a relationship between you is to work, you will have to cultivate more patience than you usually show, and be a generous and tasteful lover.

Try to accept your **7**'s obsessive cleanliness: they will not be happy living in chaos. **7** thrives in an environment that is elegant and precise. In fact, the worst problem for you to negotiate is probably that your **7** is critical of everything and everyone – especially themselves – and you are in need of 'help' in most areas on the home front, and as far as organization and method is concerned. Call in the professional services that you can afford, to keep things running – a home clean and clear of clutter. More than any other number, you need 'gentle organizers' – someone to come regularly to clean and mend, to help put things into order, or a personal assistant who will co-ordinate as an 'angel' working the necessary miracles. A **7** lover will never scold about the budget for such necessities!

Key themes

5 strains against **7**'s perfectionism, privacy requirements, solitude, and obsessive and meticulous demands • Expect a push/pull scenario, but shared communication and personal sensitivity will help!

5 in love with an 8 ★★★

When an **8** meets a **5**, other people can see the sparks flying between you. There is a buzz between the two of you, and it is exciting. You may well have met in the work arena, where your flamboyant personal styles and sheer force of character stood out from the grey backdrop behind you. You are birds of a feather, indeed. Yet you are also, perhaps, too similar for this to be a wrinkle-free ride. **8** oozes efficiency, and **5** smoulders with potential: it doesn't take clever **8** more than a moment to see this is going to be a fascinating encounter.

Your physical attraction may have opened the door, and it will probably go on working well even when other facets of your relationship stagger. **5** wants to be reckless and live wildly, and **8** wants to take control of **5**'s madness and brilliance. Of course, this could be mutually beneficial, but you're not always happy to offer another the control panel, nor is **8** going to sit back quietly and give you all the limelight for what you both achieve together. Ego clashes seem inevitable. And will it irritate you that your progressive **8** tries to do all of the jobs and become an icon of industry and achievement?

This is a problem that **8**s also share with **1** lovers; it leaves no time for your personal relationship. Tensions rise and tempers flare when you enter into personal relationships that affect both of you in business (or in business bonds that stray into your personal life). Neither you nor **8** is very good at putting up boundaries, and life may be all work and play mixed together – too high-voltage, not enough quiet time. Burn-out looms, if this is the way you conduct your relationship.

But what works works. Both of you have minds that are active, alert, thirsty for knowledge along with the rainfall. With a high degree of sexual energy and adventure, you will take your **8** lover up, up and away: they could really learn to love your spur-of-the-moment suggestions for out-of-the-way encounters. The one difficulty you will face is to get your **8** home from their place of work and into your passionate embrace. Still, you're good with words, and you should work to entice your lover and begin the seduction process earlier in the day, or even the night before. They'll love you for showing them how to release and unwind.

If you can recognize that you are both risk-takers, and try not to outdo each other – which would definitely lead to ruin! – you might join forces and make things really happen around you both. The risks are the problem. **8**s can't help attracting attention from admirers and sycophants who long for their power and glamour and vibrancy, and **5**s are simply magnetic to all. Things may spiral out of control, and you, as the **5**, will have a job reining in your **8**'s willpower.

Competitive elements are inevitable, unless you have reached the wiser end of your character. Then, it's true, the best shines out: a life of radiance and action, intellectual inquiry and physical effort. Which model are both of you?

Key themes

Lovers who enjoy style, quality and a love of luxury • Comfort and a warm atmosphere suit you both best • Frustrations occur when communication is at cross-purposes or unclear • Competition between you, or bouts of being unrealistic and unco-operative, will sour the relationship

5 in love with a 9 ★★★

With two numbers that are forever on the move, perhaps the attraction between you came about on a plane or in an international hotel? You may have glimpsed each other's smart luggage – which stood out from all others in the lobby – rather approvingly. **9**'s taste is more conventional and traditional, but you can admire that, and also draw approbation from **9** for your own ineffable signature style. Part of the magnetism between these numbers, indeed, is about energy and movement, a sense of the *possible*, a wish for cramming life with activity, thought and feeling. The travellers personified of the number-cycle, **9** and **5** are both sensory and yet philosophical, and together you have much to interest one another on a day-to-day, and month-to-month, basis.

Where you want stimulus, but have to fight many

numbers to be allowed personal freedom and opportunity, your **9** will certainly never hold you back or forbid you from trying things independently. **9** is excited by your forcefulness about life, your feeling that all experiences are for the trying. Most likely neither one of you will prejudge others because of the colour of their skin, their cultural creed or their social status. **5**s and **9**s take anyone on merit, and are prepared to be enthralled by any other human being with a tale to tell.

These common humanitarian tenets are a strong draw-card in your potential relationship, and this is part of what works well. Both of you are also bright, wilful and alert. Just as importantly, you – with all the acumen and optimism of your number – can take the sometimes moody and depressive **9** by the hand and lead them out of gloominess, as your versatility and talent for promotion can underwrite **9**'s abilities in the arts or educational arena. **9** may often prevaricate in life, with too many talents to choose from, but if anyone can make them feel their power and potential – and help them to utilize it – it will be you!

So why isn't it a five-star relationship? After **9** has been excited by **5**'s contacts and motoring power, a basic need to be a loner and live a quieter life at times may be at odds with **5**'s restlessness. **9** can be just too gloomy – feeling for the ills and pains of everyone else. You have no time for such sentiment, because your generosity and love is about positivity. **9** would be better with tender-hearted **6** than don't-slow-me-up **5**. **5** is always ready to work on cheering up a fellow life-passenger, but not going over and over the same ground. **9** can't make that cut-off point.

Then, too, in terms of expectation, you may be too much of a gambler for the more conservative **9**, who wants someone to concentrate on their needs. **9** is a missionary, a reformer, a person who is excited by achieving the wishes of others. This philanthropy may come at the expense of your time together, and may leave you feeling a little too dull and worthy. Where is the fun? But the worst problem is that neither of you has the steadiness to calm or direct the other's countless energies and creative gifts. **9** needs more of a rock than **5** can be, and **5** will appreciate a partner who can offer them space and wisdom. So, what is good is *good* between you – but the nervousness you may generate in each other could make a truly lasting relationship a little elusive.

Key themes

Both ready for change and variety in lifestyle and among friends • **9** is warm, spontaneous and unprejudiced; **5** can help **9** discover greater humour, self-expression and self-confidence • Both a little high-strung – **9** more a traditionalist, and **5** in a tearing hurry

5 in love with an 11 ★★

It's all about the way it looks to the world, this partnership! You love the splash you make, the raw sex appeal you exude as a pair, the sparkle you create together when you go out or arrive anywhere. Your **11** love is more ambitious and more driven than you are, and will discover unique ways of doing absolutely anything. Perhaps you've met your match ...

But **11**'s ups and downs, moods and energy drives, are high and low – hardly gauged to fit in with your similar dips and bursts. A competitive spirit may get in the way just a little too often, and it seems too high-voltage for either of you to be relied upon to smooth things over when one of you is under siege – which may happen so frequently. And, even creatively, both of you have such distinctive, charismatic talents that you may end up permanently trying to outdo each other. Nor is **11** likely to dissuade you from your worst streaks of risk-taking. In other words, this could get right out of control.

If the relationship between you is to work, you must try not to search for the answers to your own shortcomings in your partner: look to yourself for answers, and repair those awful misunderstandings. Shared mood swings can take their toll, and, as **5**s require variety and are people-intensive, the loner instinct in the **11** despairs. **11**s are discerning, dreamy and faithful – but it is questionable whether the variety provided within the **11**'s own complex char-acter will be enough to reform the straying, adventure-seeking **5**.

OK – so now let's look at the brilliant thing about a **5/11** partnership: neither one of you will let the other lapse into complacency. Many achievements will mark the high point of your relationship, and a shared love of danger may entice you to move ever up and on, never resting on your mutual laurels. But one thing's for sure: security will be hard to come by! Strife comes from the absolute similarity between you, and the fact that you recognize so many traits – both attractive and unattractive – in each other. Ego, eccentricity, brilliance, personal magnetism, fire, enthusiasm for life, and impatience towards more sequential thinkers – you exacerbate the best *and* the worst in one another.

You each draw admiration from your individual followers, but your **11** only knows how to lead. Sometimes this won't irritate you, but if it is forever so, you will lose your good grace about it over time. If you can somehow agree on which way it is that you both want to go, you may create a very lively paradise; but if you antagonize and disorientate one another – as seems so potentially possible – you are creating more of a nightmare.

This is a match or a mismatch, and which it is will depend on how mature and educated, philosophical and wise, you have become. If you can organize your exceptional combined talents and visions, you will be an eccentric, high-powered pair.

Key themes

Exhausting or stimulating • Dash and daring flavour all your pursuits together, but competition can be destructive • Sharing and trust must be worked at • **11** can manage their own extremes of nervousness and tension, but these are exacerbated by unpredictable **5**'s demanding and frantic energies

5 in love with a 22 ★★★★

Just as with **11**, this enchanted being attracts you powerfully – but perhaps to better lasting effect. You know quality when you see it, and your attractive **22** is cut from superior cloth, and is, in every sense, a bit special. Authoritative, calm and yet excitable, **22** offers you an anchor – someone who is unruffled, for the most part, which allows you to return to a safe harbour whenever you need to. Though the qualities of **4** are your direct opposite, the sheer force of attraction here can get past the boredom threshold for you more effectively, and allow you to feel excited by the potential of the tie. And you love anyone who stretches you or keeps you on your toes.

Your **22** is also curious about you: your style and humour, your vitality, your thirst for knowledge and experience. You admire their quiet awareness of their own basic superiority to nearly everyone else around them – and yet their surprising lack of apparent ego. What a captivating cocktail! This is someone you want to get closer to – a lover you want to slow down for, if (and only if!) absolutely necessary. This person is going somewhere, and you want to go too.

Some smaller issues are going to trouble you both: your **22** is a stickler for detail, and knows where everything is to be placed, while you are constantly in a state of chaos. You are a restless soul, forever on the run – nothing is put away, benches are not cleaned and certainly not sorted or cleared. Accounts are not paid on time, clothes are not hung up, appointments are missed, and worse – you have forgotten to fill the car up with petrol and are on your way to an important occasion ... so you are now running late. That spells disaster to your **22** – and to a long-term commitment. **5**s do not think about such trifles!

Your **22** will not be pushed around, talked over or

tricked into believing any feeble tale. You will have to accommodate their thinking on every issue, because – unlike the more compliant **4**, who is happy to let you have the credit for what you mutually achieve – this is someone who needs to be recognized, and who will stand up for what is just and right. You have a crusader in your life here, and you will be impressed by all that they do or say ... but it is a different method of 'doing' to your own. You will need to discover how generous you can be, if this is to work really well – which it may: this might just be one of those unions that inspires both parties to work through their issues, to produce a successful and personally rewarding connection.

One thing that can be a problem is that your **22** lives off quite a bit of nervous energy (unlike a **4**), and likes to work right through any project until it's done. This can mean long hours, travel commitments, late nights. At best, this gives you that valuable freedom and space you crave, but it also means you can drift apart occasionally. And overwork for both of you can bring on emotional stresses, resulting in the 'blame game'.

But, overall, this relationship has considerable potential, and may help you, as the **5**, to actualize your extraordinary talents. **22** won't settle for less!

Key themes

Colourful outbursts pepper this union • **5** is at action stations, ever ready to move and change direction, while **22** tries to pin them down to talk about the future and make a plan • Respect is key

Work

YOUR WORK COMPATIBILITY CHART

	1	2	3	4	5
With a 1	★★★★	★★★★★	★	★★★	★★★
With a 2	★★★★★	★★★	★★★	★★★★	★
With a 3	★	★★★	★★★★	★★	★★★★★
With a 4	★★★	★★★★	★★	★★★★★	★★★
With a 5	★★★	★	★★★★★	★★★	★★
With a 6	★★	★★★★★	★★★★	★★★★	★★★★
With a 7	★★★★★	★★★	★★★	★★★★★	★★
With an 8	★★★★★	★★★★★	★★★★★	★★★	★★★★
With a 9	★★★★	★★★	★★★★★	★★	★★★
With an 11	★★	★★★★	★★★	★★★★★	★★
With a 22	★★★★★	★★	★★★	★★★	★★★★

6	7	8	9	11	22
★★	★★★★★	★★★★★	★★★★	★★	★★★★★
★★★★★	★★★	★★★★★	★★★	★★★★	★★
★★★★	★★★	★★★★★	★★★★★	★★★	★★★
★★★★	★★★★★	★★★	★★	★★★★★	★★★
★★★★	★★	★★★★	★★★	★★	★★★★
★★★	★	★★★★	★★★	★★★★★	★★★★
★	★★★★	★★★	★★	★★★★	★★★★★
★★★★	★★★	★★★	★★★★	★★★★★	★★★★
★★★	★★	★★★★	★★★	★★★★★	★★★★★
★★★★★	★★★★	★★★★★	★★★★★	★★★★	★★★★★
★★★★	★★★★★	★★★★	★★★★★	★★★★★	★★★

5 working with a 1 ★★★

In an office environment, **5** and **1** can be a surprise package. The **5** is an exuberant, sometimes boundless, enthusiast for almost any original idea, which means you have someone who has already decided your concepts are good before you've even voiced them. The worry is that no one's looking at the fine print – so it would help if a **2** or a **4** is available for that! After all, if you two get going, who will stop you?

5 is a born promoter – the proverbial salesman who can take oil to Texas – and **1** comes up with the ideas worth selling. They devise it; you verbalize it. Together, you generate lively discussions and clever approaches to work, and others find you both good company and utterly positive in what you do. Moreover, you are lucky together, and give each other a boost when people around you seem flat and uninspired.

The light flashes amber when you both need the approval of a crowd, or when you feel that the **1** is taking too much merit for an achievement. You are happy with others taking their part, and may be irritated by **1**'s wish for privacy and seclusion in order to develop strategies for business. Why not talk them through? The other problem for you is accomplishing routine work, or anything demanding a long stint at one thing, or in one place. This suggests that both of you need others to fill in crucial links – people in the team, perhaps, who will soften the dynamic between two boisterous and confident people. But the pairing of a **5** and a **1** at work is clever, and you should be able to inspire each other to greater heights and fresher ideas over time.

Key themes

Zinging atmosphere • Several balls in the air • Good contact • Others required for back-up

5 working with a 2 ★

This is a tricky work relationship, because **2** doesn't understand what makes **5** tick in business – and that's unusual. **2**s have such a hold on most people's inner motives, hearing words unspoken; and perhaps therein lies the difficulty. **5** is almost never silent – always talking things up and achieving much that is extraordinary through pure chat. **2** believes this is the sign of a phoney, and doesn't trust **5**. **2** appreciates inner stillness and focus, but **5** gets by in a different world, making a splash with the perfect bon mot. By **5**'s standards, **2** is old-fashioned or over-cautious and, as in romance, it is not always easy to smooth the ruffled feathers of a **5** and a **2** working in nearly any context.

Perhaps the best chance for harmony is if you start out in a junior capacity and have to rely on your considerable charm to win the **2** over from the first. This may lead to a lasting truce, and a grudging willingness on the **2**'s part to admire a personality at work whose talents can be measured in results. **2**, then, may be quietly amused and accepting, but will hardly be converted to your cheeky, advertising-executive way. **2** would always rather do things with control, and the solid attributes of the **4** that are so suited to a **2**'s working make-up are exactly what is missing in the gambling, earthy **5**, who is never bland enough to appeal to everyone. Which is a shame, given that you might flourish with **2**'s careful hands at the wheel at times.

The best approach with these two numbers is to give them a great divide and let them deal with it as best they can. At least it will entertain everyone around them!

Key themes

Underlying tension • Two very different personalities with little overlap of method

4 3 2 1 9 8 7 6 5

5 working with a 3 ★★★★★

This is a coming together of the sports star and the photographer, or the actor and the talent agent: though which is which will occasionally be the question! **3** admires your drive and physical energy, and you really understand what **3** is on about when they go off on a flight of fancy. **5** promotes **3**'s ideas better than anybody, and **3** puts a frame around **5**'s cinematic visions. Together you achieve symmetry, your concepts overlapping well and your imagination bolstering each other. Both numbers are excellent at managing and inspiring people, and each has a feeling for the balance between what is necessary and what is enjoyable. You are, as it were, speaking the same language.

In any given sphere, and on any particular day, **5** may be **3**'s boss and **3** may be **5**'s; this is because you direct each other alternately. It may be hard to say who is more responsible for the other's success. Did **3** provide the perfect vehicle for **5**'s promotional skills? Or did **5** see a way to capitalize on **3**'s creative talents? Can **5** do without **3**'s imagination? No more than **3** could flourish without **5**'s support. In every way, you two attack things with gusto. Nothing is impossible, and you never give up or say die.

5's interests are likely to move **3**'s into new territories too, and being around both of you will be a funny and pleasurable experience for your team-mates. If there is a **4** anywhere in the grouping, they may feel left behind once you two start on your run of ideas. One needs to be quick-witted to keep up. This is an occasionally competitive, but mostly highly entertaining, effective partnership.

Key themes

Both create buzz and a sense of what is possible • Complementary skills and respect for each other's method

5 working with a 4 ★★★

If one of you can be generous to the other's very different way of attacking things, this pairing at the office could be surprisingly good. You have exactly the whirlwind of ideas and energy **4** needs to get motivated, and, once **4**'s cautious enthusiasm is added to the mix, they become the think-tank who decides whether something is ultimately achievable. Interestingly, **4** contributes to your imaginative concepts, because they ask the questions that need to be posed if a project is ever to have wings. You aren't bothered with such details – where the money will come from, or if there's a viable market. **4** is, though, and their line of enquiry will ensure that a clever idea from you is also *useful*.

But from here we may run into stormy weather, because **4** is like a snuffer to **5**'s spark. **5** functions by ignoring some of the trouble that might be ahead – very much like a **1**, rushing in where angels fear to tread. If **5** worried about teetering on the precipice, or the height from which they are going to jump, they would never perform those exciting feats that are their hallmark. **5** wants progress, and **4** consolidation – and this essential difference in the way of evaluating life is going to cause hiccups ...

Unless, of course, you can retire to opposite corners, and agree that there are horses for courses, and that each of you has a different area of excellence. **4** can find a way to bring your dream to reality, if anyone can; and you can cajole **4** out of grumpy resilience into change. So **4** can work long into the evening on a tenth cup of coffee, while you quaff champagne for inspiration ... is that a problem?

Key themes

Ideologically at odds, but have complementary skills • Requires willingness to set aside differences

4 3 2 1 9 8 7 6 5

5 working with a 5 ★★

If you find yourselves working in a team situation in the office, or on a sporting team, then the progressive, competitive energy will spur each of you on. This coupling works similarly (yet with much greater negative potential) to the **5/3** union, where there is also a disregard for practicalities, rules and personal disciplines, with a danger that very little is achieved. Just who will be the organizer, the planner, the constructive achiever in this **5/5** coupling?

Other strong core numbers – the **LIFE** number (*see page 214*), and gentle letters such as 'D's or 'O's in your names – may hold the checks and balances, so that all is not lost between you. There is enormous potential of creativity, intensity, passion for success, desire for material reward, great humour and devastating wit – so much so that life in your company could almost be a cabaret. But caution hovers, because this 'mirror-imaging' can indicate excesses, freedoms, sexual misadventure, risk-taking in all forms, resulting in scattered goals and wasted energy, lost opportunities, or senseless stagnation of creative talents. The potential for disaster must be acknowledged, and responsibility taken on board by both parties, with self-discipline potentially helping to overcome these personal hurdles.

Yet there can be a single-mindedness towards the success of any project where you pool your enormous resourcefulness and creativity toward the goal. As long as others can perform the nuts and bolts of function and process, the energy you two share – when focused toward the greater good of the outcome – could be impossible to beat.

Key themes

Team spirit must be encouraged • Must acknowledge shortcomings • Witty and wonderful, but also unreliable?

5 working with a 6 ★★★★

6 may not be quite sure of the storm that hit them the day you arrived in their work arena! Into a sea of tranquillity comes an illuminated pleasure boat, ready to liven things up; and, though this is the antithesis of what a **6** wants in their domestic life, in business it is a little bit exciting. Your **5** bombast is good for lethargic **6** – who isn't lazy, but inclined to stay out of the line of fire, frequently losing out just to avoid confrontation. You are delighted to do **6**'s verbal jousting, and will take many of their good ideas more seriously, and actualize them. And **6** – always patient and kind to all – smoothes over those wrinkles with all the clients and co-workers you have no notion you've offended.

6 can teach your brilliant ideas to other, slower, lesser mortals – something **5** is rarely bothered about – and you stir **6** to become more aggressive about possible goals. You each boast varied creative abilities – **5**'s more unconventional, **6**'s more traditional; but this means you can combine to appease just about anyone. The real blessing here is that you are opposites who will respect each other. In business, **5** recognizes **6**'s gentle, diplomatic soul, and **6** is determined to find the peace and let you have your way.

Businesses that would feed off the abilities you two share are in marketing or public services, real-estate sales and development, publishing or journalism, all of which demand original ideas but offer beauty or comfort. You will admire **6**'s exquisite taste and be grateful for their encouragement concerning your input; give them precedence in work decisions that need an aesthetic element to succeed.

Key themes

Draw inspiration from one another • Can please many parties • Co-operation essential for your progress

5 working with a 7 ★★

This is a little like the coming together of the jazz band and the classical trio! While there is little doubting your individual talents, they are diametrically opposed. **5**s are quick on the uptake, skilful, productive and progressive, while **7**s are analytical specialists, refined, logical, accurate and erudite. **7** may not be convinced by **5**'s dilettantism, distracted by the scattering force of your multifaceted energy.

At times, **7** can perfect what you create, and you may retire to opposite sides of a room and get on without interference. The **7** may have the specialist education that you admire, where you have the raw dynamic sales ability and daring they may feel they lack. Your free thinking joined to **7**'s discipline could move financial mountains, so suffice to say this union can create material satisfaction for each of you and, in this way, you can become a good team.

One of the problems is that the **7** is discerning in their outlook, selecting projects they can interest themself with. **5** is always more radical, alive to a wider group of people, keen to try something risky, where a **7** shrugs and wonders about the waste of time. **7** watches the horizon for charlatans, whereas you are beguiled and excited by the pirates and the pioneers. And, somehow, this difference grates.

Individual autonomy will help you to function simultaneously; thus you would be happiest in your own shared business, rather than working for a corporation. Potential disasters relate to **5**'s mode of attack: **7** may bristle at ill-timed flamboyance and the disarray you leave in your wake. **7** needs a tranquil space for this to succeed.

Key themes

5 produces ideas, **7** refines them • Need to understand each other's weaknesses • **7** offended by **5**'s disregard for accuracy

5 working with an 8 ★★★★

Here are a couple of potential workaholics; if you haven't taken off yet, you are both failing in your capabilities. **5** and **8** hold similarities: both of you are venturesome, progressive, resourceful, skilful, straightforward, capable and courageous. **8** never, though (unlike you), trusts to luck, but finds out exactly what is needed and provides it.

8's mind is ready to see potential in your dreams, and they know just how to actualize your business ideas. If a new project of your design requires a crash course or learning to master a previously untried discipline, **8** will do it. No one can see how your brilliant mind is working better than **8**, but they also know how to light the touch paper under you, and get you moving in a more focused direction. **8** has a humour for **5**'s madness, but takes your occasional genius very seriously. And, as **8**s are excellent managers with a disciplined financial awareness, they support and pre-empt your practical needs (and will have appointed an office manager to handle the practicalities!).

You will often need to fly by the seats of your pants, as they say: **5**s need to be reminded about sequential process and responsibility to complete what they have undertaken, but fortunately **8** has 'big business' stamped on its forehead, and expect results from you. You can't fool them, and probably won't let them down – rising to greater heights than ever under their tutelage. Be warned not to run yourselves ragged by over-reaching, or over-estimating your worth, and allow each other the freedom of your own patch, so you don't thwart one another's intentions.

Key themes

Complementary skills • **8** provides stability for **5**, and **5** responds to the goals **8** sets out for them

5 working with a 9 ★★★

Fairly well-met souls, **5** is the 'people person' and **9** the feeling humanitarian who understands colleagues' woes. What motivates each of you may be diverse: **5** is curious, spontaneous and warm, finding joy in communicating with people from all walks of life; **9** is broad-minded, compassionate and altruistic, always anxious to please others. **9**s set high standards and **5** might well respond to this.

Your optimism helps **9** get out of bed on a stressful day, and **9** has the clarity to see how to realize your ideas. You start well, and the **9** finishes for you once you lose interest. Best of all, you create a feeling of goodness in your co-workers, for **9** buoys your spirits while you stop **9** from worrying unduly. And what good ideas you come up with together – though you'll need others to do the paperwork!

You know exactly what **9** can add: you can be cold-blooded with others' ideas in a way you never manage with your own. You see when **9**'s head is too high in the clouds, and you're the one person fearless enough to say so. You are the force needed to get the **9** out of the blocks – preventing them from over-rehearsing each performance. But arguments and aggravation will scatter your energies, and the two of you may run headlong into the more negative traits of your numbers, and lose confidence or feel blocked. Acknowledge the need for discipline, and adhere to the sequential processing rule that there must be a beginning, middle and end to achieve a strong result. Have a plan and a budget, and stick to it. Keep a sense of adventure in what you do, and define your direction.

Key themes

An energized team • Intuit one another's best gifts for work • Employ a management team to polish your efforts

5 working with an 11 ★★

This could hold the promise of success, especially in relation to a student/teacher relationship – and yet the potentially clashing aspect of your personalities rates this work bond with only two stars. You both want to be the star player in any team, **5** loving centre-stage and **11** simply being the 'star'. You both have delicate egos, **11**'s more fragile, so you'll need a string of seconds to do your bidding. To you, the **11** is unstable and, to them, you're a bit rough around the edges. In a nutshell, neither of you really brings out the best in each other.

If you are truly evolved souls and have got past the competitive stage, you may be able to appreciate that you are both dynamic risk-takers with great personal courage and the capacity to work tirelessly for extended periods. **11** may be too metaphysical for your taste, seeing things in a poetic and metaphoric way, where you prefer to size them up decisively. **11** relies on intuition; your instincts are based on lightning-fast assessments of what you see, or have absorbed. You are both highly creative and genuinely inventive, so it's a pity you can't put your differences aside more often and help each other across the finishing line.

Trust is crucial to any kind of success. Share your inspirational dreams honestly, and display an understanding of your different talents, attitudes and capabilities. The best opportunities for doing well together are in the teaching professions, as both of you can be inspirational and will admire each other's achievements. Competing in business may be very trying for those around you.

Key themes

Two stars wanting top billing • Potential for learning, but **5** is impatient and **11** highly strung and discerning

5 working with a 22 ★★★★

Here is someone most people work well with, because they take the abilities of a **4** and make something more exciting from them. For you, working with a **22** is a privilege. They will rely on your powers to stir up whatever is inert and push across the frontier into new pastures. If you work with a **22**, you will be given scope to do anything and everything you can to make use of your energies and creative talents for the good of many. **22** can prevent you from offending others too, because they understand your best talents are in promotion and sales rather than negotiation – unless they need you to wake everyone up!

You have a mutual understanding of what excites one another. You realize **22** is different – a deep thinker, wanting to create a free world; they realize you have the daring and conviction to argue for that world's existence. You are the 'go-getter' that **22** needs to progress their wishes. You push the boundaries and break a few rules, and refuse to give up. Together, you have high ideals, taking a practical suggestion and making it nationally appealing.

Though cut from different cloth, you understand that there is more to your **22** colleague. In awe of real talent and superior mental skills, you understand that people who are different are so for a reason. If no one stood apart from the crowd, things would stay the same – and this would frustrate both of you. And, just when you feel you have discovered something new but no one recognizes you, your **22** ally will draw attention to your merits. Overall, this is a very positive and potentially constructive work bond.

Key themes

5 needs **22**'s meticulous capabilities, and **22** needs freeing up • Success likely and philanthropy to be encouraged

Friendship

YOUR **FRIENDSHIP** COMPATIBILITY CHART

	1	2	3	4	5
With a 1	★★★	★★★★★	★★	★★★	★★★
With a 2	★★★★★	★★	★★★	★★★★	★
With a 3	★★	★★★	★★★★	★	★★★★
With a 4	★★★	★★★★	★	★★★★★	★★
With a 5	★★★	★	★★★★	★★	★★★
With a 6	★	★★★★	★★★★★	★★★	★★★★
With a 7	★★★★	★★★★★	★★★★	★★★★★	★
With an 8	★★★★	★★★★	★★★★★	★★	★★★★
With a 9	★★★★	★★★	★★★★	★★★★	★★★★
With an 11	★★★	★★★★★	★★	★★★★★	★★
With a 22	★★★	★★★	★★★★	★★	★★★

6	7	8	9	11	22
★	★★★★	★★★★	★★★★	★★★	★★★
★★★★	★★★★★	★★★★	★★★	★★★★★	★★★
★★★★★	★★★★	★★★★★	★★★★	★★	★★★★
★★★	★★★★★	★★	★★★★	★★★★★	★★
★★★★	★	★★★★	★★★★	★★	★★★
★★★★	★	★★★★	★★★★	★★★	★★★★★
★	★★★★	★★★	★★	★★★★★	★★★★★
★★★★	★★★	★★★★	★★★★	★★★★★	★★★
★★★★	★★	★★★★	★★	★★★★	★★★★
★★★	★★★★★	★★★★★	★★★★	★★★★★	★★★★
★★★★★	★★★★★	★★★	★★★★	★★★★	★★

You get on well with a lot of people, though you will have moments of wanting peace and privacy from every single one of them! Let's see which are the best combinations ... and which are the worst:

5 and **1** (★★★): You both appreciate the side of each other's personality that offers similarities: energy, humour and a wish to get on with life. Neither of you are passive, but occasionally your restlessness is too much for **1**, and you will often fall out.

5 and **2** (★): Different styles about everything, here. **5** seems short-sighted to **2**, undervaluing things **2** feels have great merit. You may be too blasé, or not care deeply enough about people **2** thinks more deserving – but then, you may think **2** too serious and strait-laced, as well!

5 and **3** (★★★★): Instantly drawn to each other, **3** sees through your vulnerabilities and your efforts to offset them, and you have the same skill with them. Good drinking pals, you also know you are both wiser and more serious, on occasion, than the rest of the world sees.

5 and **4** (★★): Hmm. Not sure about this. Rating a mere two stars, you may be better friends than this if you are physically hardy and the **4** is at the more creative end of the scale. Usually, though, your nervous energy makes **4** ill, and **4** stretches your thin patience. Patchy.

5 and **5** (★★★): You appreciate each other's similarities: adventure-seeking, freedom-loving, alert, sensuous, creative, you share humour and a wish to get on with life. However, **5**'s trademark restlessness can mean you won't stand still long enough to hear each other properly, resulting in arguments that are, essentially, a battle of wills.

5 and **6** (★★★★): Your **6** friends have a style and gentleness which you can admire, but it's not your cup of tea. Their lives seem too staid for you, and they find you too self-indulgent and restless. But if you're in need, guess who'll be there with you? Your perfect **6** friend.

5 and **7** (★): You both come from entirely different directions: the **7** is intense and highly intellectual, while you're the spontaneous people-loving adventurer. The **7** needs to tell you honestly how they feel about you, and, depending on your degree of sensitivity, you can take it from there.

5 and **8** (★★★★): Here's a stable relationship you can rely on, with a strong sense of family ties. You share physical energy, humour, a drive for adventure, and may share sporting interests, or have been friends since school days. Watch careless comments about each other's relations and, when arguments arise, expect to feel frustrated.

5 and **9** (★★★★): Another good friendship. You understand how to drive **9** out of too much maudlin contemplation or moodiness, and they are honest with you, which you like, and appreciate your zany sense of humour. Don't hurt them with your sharp words; this is one thing they can't forgive.

5 and **11** (★★): You are attracted to each other's originality, creativity, vision and progressive spirit, but you tend to tread on each other's toes, because **5** shines out when given the limelight, but **11** also wants – expects – to be the 'star'. This friendship is interesting and equally testing!

5 and **22** (★★★): You admire and feel drawn to **22**, but intrinsic differences can lead to problems. You'll get on brilliantly with some **22**s, not at all with others, depending on other present numbers. Goal-orientated and productive, **22** can provide you with the advice you need to complete your efforts, and will be a supporting friend.

5 IN OTHER PLACES

So what does it mean when your number turns up on a house? Do you live in a 5 home? And how does the number 5 affect your pet – or even the car that you drive? Numbers exude a subtle influence on everything in our lives; and here are just a few examples of how ...

A 5 address

If the number of your address – or of your apartment – reduces back to a **5**, your home will have a 'busy' sign hanging at the entrance. If you own this home, perhaps you rent it out; or, if you do live there, you are forever travelling, or may be forced to sell it, shortly after moving in. Expect changing conditions, and, if you're sharing with flatmates, don't expect to see the same faces for long.

Having said this, it is a good investment, because it holds an attraction for the public. If it's your first home, it could be the most perfect den: quite simply, it's the ideal place to hold your youthful memories. It's not a perfect family home; if it *does* happen to be such, you may have difficulty with communications, litigation, or your children may struggle to concentrate on their tasks. This home can be unusual and dishevelled, even chaotic, for a family. But, forewarned is forearmed, as they say!

A 5 pet

If you don't know your pet's birthday, use the first letter of their name to calculate their number. If it's E, N or W, they're a **5**. This is the animal you take on if you've been told to get a dog so that you can keep fit, or lose weight; you and this pet will be on the move! This dog or cat is ready for action – your original 'happy soul', yowling and mewing. They are communicating their need for 'walkies' or games, with their lead on or a shoe between their jaws, tail wagging, ever impatient to get out of that door.

The **5** cat is up for some mischief, jumping on to (or into!) everything. And, if this is your equine friend, best make sure that the gate is high enough – and bolted! – because this animal wants to gallop and jump, and is up for any adventure ride you can manage. They'll need a stablemate, though, whether a cat, dog or duck (I have even heard that some thoroughbred **5**s favour piglets or birds!).

A 5 car

If the numbers of your licence plate reduce to **5**, this colourful vehicle is probably well-travelled or imported – and maybe pre-loved? Have you remembered to apply the brakes? Good! This little character is so anxious for action that it may be ready to take you there before you are. Perhaps your **5** is a wagon – perfect to transport you and your gaggle of pals to wherever you choose at a moment's notice. Be prepared for a wonderful adventure – flying along, laughter bouncing off the other cars as you roar by.

If this motor car of yours is small – too small for a gang of friends – then it is almost certainly a red sports car. Convertible, perhaps? It's fast and so much fun for you, but remember to visit the garage for check-ups – air in the tyres, water in the radiator – because no matter what you have in mind, your humorous little **5** vehicle is ready to rock and roll.

YOUR LIFE NUMBER
Your lesson to learn

The time has come to consider the other main number in your numerology chart: your Life Lesson, or LIFE, number. This is sometimes also called the 'Birth Force'. Just as for the DAY number, calculating your LIFE number is easy: simply add together each digit of your full birth date (day, month and year), and keep adding the digits until they reduce to a single number (*see example on page 270*).

And that's it. You have your Life number. So what does it tell us?

What does it mean?

The **LIFE** number takes times to show its mark. You should see its influence over many years, and understand that it is representative of certain strengths and weaknesses that we learn to live with through years of experience. These characteristics need to be analysed over time, and it can take a while for us to come to know ourselves truly from our **LIFE** number. Uncovering these aspects of our character is a process of discovery, and we often don't fully recognize the traits of this number as clearly, or as quickly, as those of the stronger **DAY** number.

Once you have done your sums and discovered this second important number, you'll want to find out what this means. If your **LIFE** and **DAY** numbers are the same, this powerfully reinforces the qualities of your own number, and accentuates both strengths and weaknesses. You won't be fighting corners within your personality by having two numbers to live with that are, perhaps, miles apart in spirit. But then, equally, if your numbers are the same you may lack a broad vision of the world, seeing with very sharp eyes through just a single (though enormous!) window.

On the following pages we will examine what your **DAY** number **5** is like in tandem with each other number, beginning with the powerful doubling of **5 DAY** and **5 LIFE**, and then moving on through all other possible combinations. If you discover you have a **LIFE** number which totals **11** or **22**, before it reduces to a final single digit of **2** or **4**, read the entry for **5** and **2**, or **5** and **4**, but also pay special attention to any extra information given relating to the added significance of the number being a variation of a master number.

SAME **DAY** AND **LIFE** NUMBER

With 5 as your predominant number, you are incredibly blessed with an enormous zeal for life. There is an energy with which 5 does everything that is both fascinating and irritating. There's never a project too big, or a job too hard: with a double 5, reining yourself in and focusing your incredible energy on just one task is your primary problem. Remember that mere mortals cannot always keep up with your fast pace and enthusiasm, and, while your brain may have whizzed ahead at 150 mph, the rest of us are still standing at the starting line!

Smooth operator

Possibly the sexiest of all of the numbers, **5** as both your DAY *and* LIFE number makes you unquestionably a sexy temptress or a smooth mover. With a seemingly effortless affability, you are the silent envy of many around you. It might be those legs of yours, which go all the way up, or the seamless way you throw on your clothes, that turns you into an idol. Far from being one to follow the crowd and fit yourself into the current fashions, you *are* the trendsetter. If your nail polish is chipped, then you can be sure that by the end of the day every other woman in the office will have chipped nail polish too. And, while your colleagues scrimp and save for the newest BMW, you are sleek and very much your own person, in a vintage classic or a VW Beetle convertible.

Double trouble?

You maintain that allure of *cool*, which made you popular at school, while still very much following the beat of your own drum. Not one to care about what others say, your double **5** makes you doubly stubborn – and woe betide the person who crosses you on a topic of passion! Those around you envy your laid-back attitude, but this can sometimes be a burden for **5**: finding the energy to start a project has never been your problem, but maintaining the concentration to see it through to the end is not your strong point. For you, doing something you find easy is fun for a while, but anything that does not come to you immediately is too boring to attempt.

Sometimes your stubborn **5** can stab itself in the foot by being unbending at the wrong time, and your sense of pride is such that admitting you're wrong is just not an option. This is especially true for you, as those two **5**s together can sometimes mean that you would rather wallow in being cross than actually get up and solve the problem. You have to be especially careful of this, given **5**'s incredible potential (particularly in the arts), as it can be frustrating for those around you to watch the self-destruction when you fail to utilize the talents that come easily to you. While others struggle to work the new computer programme, or to master that difficult Sudoku game, you have already finished, and are bored at the thought of having to show them how.

Lust for life

Your mostly charming and easy-going character means that fitting into new situations is no problem for you, but you don't always enjoy *positives* from your somewhat scatterbrained approach to life. You have such an esprit for life, and the living of it, that the incredible stories you tell your grandchildren will only be believable because *you* have told them. From hanging out with Mick Jagger to dinner with Mickey Mouse, there is nothing that your alluring **5** personality could tell us that we wouldn't believe. Indeed, we're quite certain it's all true!

By far one of the most frustrating combinations for those around you, you are effortlessly elegant and annoyingly attractive, yet often can't be bothered to dress with the lights on (undoubtedly how the grunge trend was first started, by one of your fellow **5**s!). You find some hard things easy, but won't consider wasting your time on anything dull. There are myriad things you could have succeeded at, and your life adventure will make quite a book – but be sure to rein in that renegade **5** fecklessness, and focus on one thing at a time. A messy desk may well be easier, but not when it hinders you making that all-important meeting, or returning that phone call to the head of Virgin Records.

Two **5**s make you an international charmer, friends with everyone from the Dalai Lama to the members of the local football team. With so much energy, anything you turn your hand to is bound to succeed; but remember to get a business partner who can handle banality, while you focus on the creative side. An enviable sex kitten or heart-throb to the day you die, life is most definitely a party when you're a **5 DAY** and **LIFE** number on a mission!

DIFFERENT **DAY** AND **LIFE** NUMBERS

Most of us will find that we have two different birthday numbers, and this can be an advantage. One number may soften the single track of the other, and mean we can see other people's viewpoints more easily. At other times, though, the numbers may be in real conflict – and this leads to vacillation in our reactions to everyday situations, or confusion about why we want to run one way and then another.

In the following pages you will discover how your own two numbers are likely to work together, and what you can do to maximize the potential of both when they are paired up.

5 Day with 1 Life

Two numbers full of drive, a **5** and **1** working together will push you to over-achieve in life. You are more hot-headed than any other **5** combination, but you have more versatility and charisma, too. **5** and **1** are the best numbers for ideas and being quick off the mark, and full of action. Both numbers have a sharp intelligence, and are naturally curious and driven to investigate what is what. Neither likes to sit around waiting for life to knock on the door.

The worst attribute of these numbers together is that impulsiveness and discontent about the way things are is likely to be acute. Also, this number combination bestows a rashness that often erupts as stinging or cruel words directed towards anyone you find slow-witted or dull in temperament. You are critical, and dissatisfied with numerous things, and this can only be remedied if you force yourself not just to dream up improvements and revisions, but actually *implement* them.

You are very physical, probably good at sport, and you enjoy being a spectator of sport, too. The two numbers direct you to travel and see the world, and to expand your work radius as far as you can. You are bound to be appointed as a speaker at whatever you do, and to be a public relations person or a front-of-house executive. And, you may work hard and long, and not mind odd hours – for both the **5** and the **1** drive you to variety, and away from being tied down.

This can be a problem in your private life, though, for the **5** side of your nature wants its freedom, and the **1** likes its independence. There is obviously space here for things to go wrong, and for misunderstandings to occur with your partners. However, these are energetic and exceptionally creative numbers, and both of them want to cover the canvas that is life with a colourful splash. In other words, you may make mistakes and offend some people, but they'll certainly know you were here!

You have a distinctive style, a particular preference for the modern over the antique when it comes to decoration of your home, and a feel for what will be important in the days to come. **5** is ultra-modern, and helps that innovative **1** imagination to fire on all cylinders. Watch your tendency to over-indulge, though, as the demands and pressures you place yourself under are likely to need release, and over-drinking or overeating can become a problem. You may also be unable to avoid the temptation to have more than one love interest – partly because an unconventional lifestyle puts you in odd places. Consider what may be counter to your eventual happiness.

5 Day with 2 Life

Two birthday numbers which are a little at odds, the marriage of **5** and **2** in your personality will make you unpredictable to many – even yourself! **5** asks you to live life to the full, to make a splash and go after what you want, whereas **2** can be shy and more personally retiring. **2**'s good sense and lack of self is quite different to **5**'s sexy personal style – its instinct to say and do what it wants, and laugh at those who don't approve. **2** would rather be a lot less trouble, and retire into the background. So which number will dominate?

The **DAY** number will always be the first to express itself, but, in the case of these two numbers, it's likely that you will feel introverted one minute and quite outgoing the next – so life around you will never be dull, or run to a guaranteed course! **5** adds energy and momentum to **2**, pushing you to speak up when you feel something strongly – which you so often do. And **5**'s ability to put things into words and finish every sentence with a quip can be good for **2**, as the **2** gives you such insight into people and situations. The effect of both numbers can therefore be entertaining as well as frighteningly on the ball.

5 lends you physical strength and a healthy dose of hardiness. Also, the effect of **5** with **2** intensifies your powers of sexual attraction and, quite probably, your physical appetite in relationships. Across the pattern of your life, as you get older, the **5 DAY** number will have an invigorating impact, for **2** is prone to nervousness and headaches – even to illness caused from emotional upsets. **5** does much to lessen the effect of emotions on your health – although you will undoubtedly live off quite an amount of nervous energy as a legacy from both numbers. Be careful about wearing yourself thin at times, when you feel particularly charged sensually or very much in love;

you will give your all and suffer the consequences later, for **5** is daring and **2** can have the propensity for extremes. Mostly, though, through many little spills and thrills, the **2** calms the chaos of **5**, while the **5** makes suppliant **2** a little more demanding.

You may have a distinctive style, with a modulated appreciation for what is traditional whipped up by a preference for more modern design. Your **DAY** number likes what is new, and **2** can be very happy with clean lines and muted colours, so your taste will have an interesting edge and always amaze the people around you. Sometimes what excites you will surprise you – the lightning bolt of feeling you get from **5** making your **2** side more adventurous. **5** shakes you up a bit, and helps you take chances in every way. This is especially good for you intellectually, and you could be very progressive and inspiring to your family, and to those who listen to you at work.

5 Day with 3 Life

For most of us, the very idea of such a supply of energy bound up in one person would make us faint. You are the showbiz committee and the booked act all in one go! Will you ever delegate? The biggest danger from having these two birthday numbers is that you will wear yourself thin, burn the candle at both ends – or any other metaphor that conveys the sense of someone packing their life with ideas and activities from dawn till dusk, and from the cradle to the grave.

You are very independent and value your freedom, and you love to get out in the world and participate in the symphony that is life. Far from urging you to concentrate on one stream of activity, you are actually at your best when you have many irons in the fire. You are impatient, restless, energetic, and have a low boredom threshold, so anyone who shares your life should be ready for an amusement park permanently erected in the back garden!

You always keep things moving, and **3**'s gift of the gab is taken to full measure when married with **5**'s vivid ability to produce quotable aphorisms. You will never spend unnecessary time getting banal things done, and you will chafe at the bit if you are forced into routine situations, because your destiny is to be both progressive and versatile, and to go boldly where none have dreamed of going before. Sometimes this makes you foolhardy, but nine times out of ten you will achieve the impossible, and leave others open-mouthed in your wake.

A comfortable home for a **5/3** will have a telephone in every room, a high-speed internet connection and a television in the kitchen. In fact, there is probably a radio in your shower, for you are always listening to what others have to say, engaging in it, and disagreeing constantly. You have an inability to finish all of the many tasks that you have on the go, and your mind is always on the next job. For the most part, though, you exude such authority that other people become inveigled in your plans and find themselves carrying out the banalities for you. It is a talent, but one you will not always be admired for.

5 and **3** heighten each other's creative talents. It is almost inconceivable that, with these numbers, you would not paint, write, sing and/or dance, have an excellent eye for photography, and make anything that is normally routine much more unusual. **5** with **3** also brings out a talent for legal matters, civil service issues and any other facets of business that require a feeling for documentation. In short, this **DAY/LIFE** combination will make such a splash in this world that the rest of us should be sure to give you the whole pool.

5 Day with 4 Life

With these numbers, the term 'organized chaos' springs to mind! **5** loves to paint life in brighter colours, take risks and try everything it can. This level of thrill is almost unimaginable to an ordinary **4**, but **5** has an electrifying effect, and makes **4**'s trademark caution seem as though it cannot be true. Although ...

The truth is that both numbers still work at full force – **5** tearing at your soul to be freer and keep on the move, and **4** asking that you secure your life against the damage that may come from high winds blowing. But, with **5** playing the part of these high winds, you may either be your own worst enemy at times, or your own best breath of fresh air. These numbers are truly at odds, and as a result you may feel tugged one way in life and then the other, not knowing quite why your energy and your mood seem to dip and swing so strongly.

At best, you are more strongly independent thanks to **4**, but value your freedom thanks to **5**, and you will get out in the world and enjoy life after a little good planning. **5**'s love of travel married to **4**'s inclination for research and fact-gathering makes you both a good linguist and an ideal travel-industry worker. Long hours won't bother you, and you will emit an aura of excitement and confidence that will win others over.

You are likely to be more impatient, thanks to your **5** **DAY** number, and also generally more restless and energetic, with a lower boredom threshold. But you are also more adventurous, which offsets probably the worst factor of number **4** – that it prefers to sit back and observe much of life without actually taking the risk to get involved. **5** sees off such conservatism. You will still take care of the banal things of life – which is good for a **5**, who often refuses such dross and expects someone else to do it – but you are also willing to stand up for your rights and go after what you want without grumpy resignation.

These numbers are not easy bedfellows, but the **5** has a stirring effect on **4**, and will encourage you, over time, to act on the talents you know you have, persuading you not to hide your light under a bushel. The plodding nature of **4** is plugged into a new electricity socket, and a whirlwind of activity could result!

5 Day with 6 Life

It would be hard to find two more different numbers! While **5** wants a constant party with a live jazz band and an open bar, **6** wants a night at the opera. **6** requires peace and tranquillity, while **5** insists that the party never stops. The conflict of these two numbers means that you have two very different sides to your personality. On the one hand, your **DAY** number makes you a fantastically enthusiastic party-lover who is friends with everyone, completely laid-back and loving of life. But on the other hand, that **6** side of your personality means that you often require quietude, and like to be given the time to focus your attention on gentler activities without interruption.

This combination makes for an explosive person whom everybody loves and admires. Added to **5**'s drive and artistic flavour, **6** brings balance and *sense* to every action. **6** anchors the frenetic **5**, ensuring that projects become achievable and jobs are more likely to get finished. **6** gives you the steadiness for business – which **5** needs to make things happen. Your party-planning business is the best around, with **5**'s unquestionable flair for colour, life and crowd-pleasing details combined with **6**'s good taste and calm business head. However, **6** can be a particularly stubborn number at times, and, while **5** makes the somewhat unbending **6** a little less uptight, **5** can be just as demanding and unrelenting when pushed. This means that it is not uncommon for you to be less laid-back than other **5**s, and surprisingly wilful and unmoving.

6 sobers **5**'s sometimes wacky fashion sense and, instead of wearing outfits for effect, ensures that you are always beautifully turned out. Though **6** is often the rambunctious **5**'s saving grace, you can be indecisive, torn between the outrageous decision and the pragmatic one. **6** soothes **5**'s temper in a crisis, giving you a more level head while other **5**s erupt around you. And **5**'s affability combined with **6**'s diplomatic skills makes you a very loyal and helpful person to know. Yet, the **5**'s inability to try things that bore them sometimes comes into conflict with **6**'s grafting attitude.

An extremely talented cook, and both useful and willing at DIY, great pleasure is taken in working on anything creative with your hands. Being left alone to re-shelf a pantry would be an ideal weekend activity for a **5/6**, who enjoys the achievement of work in the home as well as the tranquillity of time alone. The conflicting numbers also mean you love the quietude of the country but still feel the beat of the urban grind in your blood, and **5**'s friendliness puts **6**'s penchant for hospitality to perfect use.

5 Day with 7 Life

A lethal mix of quick wit and sharp tongue can occasionally make **7** an unpopular number, but here **5** spares **7** the criticism of others, and instead the qualities of both numbers combine to produce a developed and entertaining raconteur. The sociable, party-loving **5** lightens **7**'s sometimes over-analytical personality, making you a must for every dinner party and cocktail do in town. **7**'s shrewd intelligence sometimes puts **5**'s creativity on a backburner, but the two together make you an acute critic and a great admirer of art, literature and music.

LIFE 7 gives **DAY 5** far more focus than you would usually expect, and others may find the intensity with which you do things both terrifying and enticing. **5** does everything, knows everyone and is seen everywhere, and typically has fantastic creative ideas and is then bored of them by the time the next course has arrived. **7**'s enviable determination utilizes **5**'s ability to do so many different things, and channels **5**'s often excessive energy towards truly useful projects, rather than seeing it dissipated. **7** is a very private number, often mulling over decisions for many days, while **5** is an extrovert. **5**'s often surprising stubbornness fuels **7**'s inclination to brood, and it is not uncommon for **5** to furiously voice the comments that **7** might ordinarily keep under wraps – but with such humour!

7 provides **5** with the drive to succeed at one thing until it is done: **7** detests dilettantism, and instead forces your often unruly **5** side to direct itself towards reaching the very highest levels of its potential. **5**'s passionate and sexy personality combined with **7**'s frighteningly high standards means that serious love relationships will not always be easily found, but fervent office affairs make you a vixen or a sex god not to be trifled with. Your reputation is one of envied ruthlessness – **7**'s intolerant nature roused by **5**'s surplus energy – making you both a feared opponent and a revered colleague.

Often the **5/7** combination channels **5**'s creativity into **7**'s serious talent for writing and analysis, and back again through **5**'s gift of the gab. An eye for aesthetics means that your house is perfectly laid out and designed. Yet, sometimes **7** can be too clinical, overshadowing **5**'s freer personality; be sure to let all of your **5** warmth out, and don't *always* be ruled by more serious **7**. It is sometimes hard for people to get close to you – given the high standards you set for those around you – but knowing you well is both an education and a privilege.

5 Day with 8 Life

Wow! **5** and **8** make a beautiful pairing. **5** is sociable and entertaining, with an eye for the slightly eccentric things in life, while **8** is socially skilled par excellence. The combination of these two numbers makes you an unquestionable success in business. With two such similar numbers, the parts of **5** and **8** which complement each other mean you're a fascinating and exciting person to be around. **5**'s love of partying combined with **8**'s effortless command of any situation means that – for you – the after-office hours are as much about thrilling business matters as those spent in the boardroom. **8**'s subtle awareness of others' feelings allows **5**'s flair for mixing any set of people together to shine even more – making you the host or hostess of the year on many occasions.

5 has an eye for colour, design and the arts, but **8**

channels this creativity into more tangible properties with more intellectual applications – often writing, or television. Whenever your **5** side is feeling laid-back or uninspired, **8** can rescue you, and help you to carry on till late to finish a piece of work, or take on extra work when necessary. **8** has a propensity to worry about things that the **5** would consider out of your hands, and there is occasionally a devil and an angel on your shoulder, arguing pragmatism against spontaneity. Sometimes **8** can be too hard on itself, though, and **5** helps to remind you of the good things in your life, just kicking back and relaxing being just what **5** does best.

5/8 makes an affectionate pair of numbers, though you may be equally bold – and sometimes intimidating – about love. **5** is a sexual feline waiting to pounce, while **8** seems frighteningly together – so much so that potential partners are sometimes scared off by the thought of such a precocious and unnerving lover. **5**s value their independence and this sometimes makes relationships difficult, yet **8** wants to be loved by an equal. You are torn between the attraction to partners who are driven and independent like yourself, and to those who need you around.

With **5**'s impatience and **8**'s high mind, you have no time for those who aren't keeping up with you. **5** always moves ahead quickly, frustrating those around them, and this is exacerbated by **8**'s need to keep progressing at all times. Idiots are not tolerated by either of these numbers. **8**'s drive to get on with life can sometimes blind **5**'s need for fun – but don't let it. Others love the charming, sociable person you are, and there is nothing in this world that could make you take your eye seriously off the ball for long – even if it tried.

5 Day with 9 Life

The good thing for you is that **9** is the last number, so you simply must see things through to the end. This is such an asset for **5**, who often picks up a thousand different things and never finishes one of them. You really have the ability to take a fantastical project and see it through to completion – and that is such a gift for someone with a **5 DAY** number. However, just as **5** is good at so many things, so is **9**! You may bite off an awful lot to chew on. You could find it hard to decide what direction you are going to take with your life, as you excel so easily at such a diverse range of things.

5 is always a party animal, seen at all the social events and desired by all who meet them. Yet **9** gives a new depth to **5**'s personality, making you acutely aware of how people are feeling and what support they need. **9** always picks the perfect present and has an eye for the unusual, ensuring the gift will be talked about for years. **5** is such an exciting number that really creates sunshine around you, and – coupled with **9**'s extraordinary people skills – you bring out the sunshine in everyone else as well. **9** is charitable and forgiving where **5** is rash and hot-headed, but **5**'s affability makes **9**'s offers of charity easily acceptable. **9** mellows **5**'s constant energy, and gives the rambunctious number clearer vision in the face of adversity.

9 itself brings friends and admirers, which the sexy **5** handles to perfection: you leave a path of fascination in your wake! Yet love is not always easy for the determined but tempestuous **5**, who is so adored by so many (too many?). **9** softens **5**, helping you to be seen by those around you as the person you really are, not just as the image that others have formed of the intoxicating but also exasperating **5**. Everyone wants a piece of **5** – their style, their humour and their infectious attitude towards life.

Sensible, well-mannered **9** alters this shallow image, and makes you more accessible and more beloved, helping you to see a bigger picture.

Your **9 LIFE** number adds generosity and compliance, while **5** reminds you to keep time for your own needs. While **9** alone would simply buy an adventure holiday for their friends, **5** makes you take the holiday yourself – and ensures that you have the fetching beachwear to get you noticed at the same time! Have fun with the **5** side of your nature, and don't always allow **9** to be the giver but never the recipient. As **5** would say, life is for the living and not just the giving.

THE FUTURE

Take a look what's in store...

And now we come to the calculation of your future. Each year, on your birthday, you move into a new sphere of number-influence which governs that year. The numbers progress in cycles of nine years; after nine years, the cycle starts over again, and a whole new period of your life begins afresh. The cycle can be applied to every number, so you can discover what the main issues will be for partners, friends and family, as well as for yourself, in any given year (*see calculation instructions, opposite*). Emphasis is placed on what will happen to you when you are in your own year number – that is, in any '5' year cycle.

Working out your cycle

To find out what year you're currently in, use the same formula employed for calculating the **LIFE** number, but substitute the current year for the year in which you were born. Every year, the cycle then moves on by one more number until, after a **9** year, returning to **1**, to begin the cycle again.

Calculation example 1

BIRTHDAY:	14 February 1966
TO CALCULATE THE CURRENT YEAR NUMBER:	1+4+2+[2+0+0+7 (CURRENT YEAR)]= 16, and 1+6 = **7**

*This means that on 14 February 2007 you move into a **7** year. On 14 February the following year, this would then move into an **8** year (1+4+2+2+0+0+8 = 17, and 1+7 = **8**), and the year after that, a **9** year, and so on.*

Calculation example 2

BIRTHDAY:	23 August 1981
TO CALCULATE THE CURRENT YEAR NUMBER:	2+3+8+[2+0+0+7 (CURRENT YEAR)] =22, and 2+2 = **4**

This means that on 23 August 2007 you move into a **4** *year. On 23 August the following year, this would then move into a* **5** *year (2+3+8+2+0+0+8 = 23, and 2+3 =* **5***), and the year after that, a* **6** *year, and so on.*

Many numerologists feel that the impact of a year number can be felt from the first day of that year – in other words, from 1st January. However, the usual school of thought is that the new number cycle is initiated *on your birthday itself*, and my experience tends to corroborate this. So, if your birthday is fairly late in the year – November or December, say – this means that you will have gone through most of the calendrical year before *your* new number-year cycle for that year begins.

Look back over some recent years, and see if – in the descriptions on the following pages – you can pinpoint the moment when your yearly number-cycle for any given year became apparent. You'll be amazed at just how accurate this system seems to be.

A 1 year

This is the perfect time to set up new and quite specific long-term goals, and consider just where you want to be a few years from now. You will have new people around you from this point on, and fresh ideas about them and the interests they awaken in you. This is a completely new chapter in your life, and you should set goals for a better and more fulfilling future.

Career-wise, a **1** year often occurs at a time of new employment, or of a complete change in direction in your working life. You are probably wanting to develop new skills or make use of untested talents. You have to believe in yourself now. This is the time when it's a little easier to step back and see how to get started along a particular path. Goals, you will understand, are perfectly attainable, even if a year ago they seemed unrealistic. In a **1** year you have tremendous focus and independence, and excellent determination.

The secret to your success now is in your ability to concentrate; but, emotionally, things can be quite testing. No matter how strong a love bond may be in your life, a **1** year demands that you do much for yourself. You could feel isolated or unsupported, even if someone dear is close by. This is a test of your own courage and inner strength. Only your strongest desires will gain results ... but then, your desires should be fierce during this cycle. Try not to act impulsively, as the push to do so will be powerful, but also, don't be afraid to be independent and go your own way. Strong urges are driving you – forward, for the most part – and a **1** year lends you exceptional clarity and energy.

A 2 year

A year which demands co-operation and partnerships at every level, **2** is a gentle year cycle, when you can consolidate what you started in the previous twelve months. You will need to be diplomatic and sensitive towards other people's feelings, but your intuition is very strong now, and you are able to share the load and the initiative more than you were allowed last year. For this reason, don't try to push things too far or too fast. After the previous whirlwind year, this is a moment to take your time and get things right.

Relationships come more into focus during a **2** year. This is especially pleasing if someone new entered your life in the last year or so, for the vibration of **2** helps a bond to strengthen, and a feeling of mutuality improves now. In some ways you may feel the desire or the need to be secretive, but this is because there are unknown elements at work all on fronts. It will affect you at work and at play, and in a close tie you will discover new tenderness that will probably separate you from other friends. If there is no one special currently in your life, this may be the year to find someone: a **2** year brings a relationship much stronger than a fling!

Your negotiation skills and ability to guess what another person is feeling may work very well for you this year; and, if the number **2** derives from master number **11** (which it almost surely will), there is a chance for serious partnerships and master opportunities. You will need to look at contracts carefully, and spend time on legalities. But this is often the most exciting and unusual year out of the nine. Mysteries come to light, and your ideas flow well. Just be prepared to consider another person in every equation.

A 3 year

Time for you! This twelve-month period is concerned with developing your abilities and testing your flexibility. Your imagination is especially strong, and you may have particular opportunities to improve your wealth and make lasting friendships. You will also need to be focused, because the energy of a **3** year is fast and furious, and may make you feel dissolute. Usually, though, this is a happy year spent with some travel prospects and many creative inspirations. Difficulties which intruded in the previous two years are often resolved in this year cycle.

Business and your social life often run together in a **3** year, and work will be a lot of fun. It is worth taking time over your appearance and indulging yourself more than usual, for the sociability of this number brings you many invitations and a chance to create a new look, or to explore other aspects of your personality. You have extra charm this year, so try to use it where it is needed.

Many people find that the number **3** expresses itself in a year cycle as a third person to consider: frequently, this is the birth of a child or an addition to the family, but it might be that another party pressures you in your personal relationship. Don't talk too much about this, or show nervousness. Under a **3** vibration, it is easy to become exhausted – even through over-excitement – so be alert to the impulse towards extravagance and fragmentation. Try to enjoy the way in which you are being drawn out of yourself this year, and allow yourself time to study, write, paint. Anything you really want you can achieve now – even strange wishes and desires can be pulled towards you. Make sure you think a little about what you are asking for!

A 4 year

A much-needed year of good-housekeeping – on the personal level, as well as literally. This year will demand practicality from you. Often a **4** brings a focus on money or accounts, on repairs around the home, or on putting your life into better order. It may not be what you want, yet it will force itself upon you. It is sometimes a year spent with a pen in hand – writing lists or cheques, doing sums and keeping diaries. It is also a year when you will need to do some research, to find out about what you don't know.

You have so much work to do in a **4**, or **22**, year – more than for a long time. Your personal pleasure takes second place to requirement, and it may seem difficult to stick to the task sometimes. Money demands that you do so, for extra expenditure is not advised in this twelve-month period. Yet, if this sounds stressful, it also gives you a feeling of satisfaction that you will achieve so much this year – a job of hard work and dedication really well done. It may be that this year gives you a very good foundation for the future and sets up lasting improvements.

You will never survive a **4** – or, especially, a **22** – year if you are not organized and implement a system of work and life. Be honest in what you do with others, but also in what you do for yourself. You cannot deceive yourself, and must check details carefully. You may have a feeling of burden at times, but there is a chance to feel you have done something extraordinary, too. Translate your clever ideas into practical results. The most significant thing for you to do is to concentrate on proper personal management. The weight of the world is on your shoulders, but you can bear it if the preparations you make are good. There is no escape from demands on your time and intelligence, but nothing can be hurried, so face the job ahead and you will soon find you have climbed a hill to new vistas.

A 5 year

After careful management of your time last year, and a feeling of being tied to the wheel, this will seem like bursting from the inside of a darkened room into bright light. Now you have a change from routine to madness, and you may feel a personal freedom that was denied you last year. Nevertheless, nothing is completely settled in a **5** year, and this uncertainty may take its toll. Try to look at this cycle as a chance to find success in newer areas, and a way to advance from necessary stagnation into running waters of energy and vitality. You will update your sense of yourself during this period, and make progress towards the life you want, following the previous year's required self-discipline.

You are admitting to the need for new pastures, so your ideas of what your life might include, or who may have a role in it, may alter now. No one likes to be held back in a **5** year, least of all you, but it is still important not to be too hasty in your actions. Use your energies, by all means, but govern them with your head. This is the time for innovation, and new takes on old goals, but if you quarrel with those dear to you, or with whom you work, it may be difficult to repair later. If change is still inevitable, be as constructive as possible, and make sure you aren't leaping from one difficult situation straight into another. You need to discover your versatility and personal resourcefulness to get the best out of this cycle. And, for some of the twelve months, travel or lots of movement seems inescapable.

This, your own number year, is potentially some kind of turning point. Learning how to adapt to sudden circumstances is vital, because any plans set in stone will cause you pain, and possibly come unstuck. Be prepared for changes and, if this brings a nervousness with it, try to meet the adventure head-on. If you talk yourself up and take on a front-running position, you can work wonders in a **5** year.

A 6 year

Love is in the air. Other things seize your time too – your home needs attention, and duties demand your energy – but, principally, this year is about emotions and relationships. Sometimes love and happiness are a reward for surviving so much in the past two years, and for unselfish service and support for others. The emphasis is on finding harmony with others, and this may come in various ways. This year, you may have the impetus and opportunity to erase problems that have previously beset you. You understand, and feel acutely sensitive towards, others, and are more radiant and beautiful than you have been for some time. If you can be kind and positive in emotional dealings, you will benefit in many ways, including materially.

There are hurdles in a **6** year in connection with obligations you feel towards others. At times you are stretched, because there are personal desires and ties you want to nurture which are countermanded by the duties you are subjected to. You may resent this, yet, if you can remain cheerful, you will be rewarded in ways not immediately apparent. Love is trying to sweep you off your feet, but your health may suffer because you are trying to fit in so much, and the intensity of your feelings is strong.

While it's good to be helpful in a **6** year, don't allow yourself to be taken advantage of, or let people drain you completely. Set up a system that lets you delegate some responsibility. Your home may bloom while you're in such a happy mood, and you should feel creative and mellow. The events of a **6** year are not as fast and furious as the previous year, but things move steadily towards a happier state of being. Let the time go as it will, because this is not a year to fight against what comes to you; get into the right philosophical gear and open yourself to pleasant surprises that come from being useful, and being warm with others.

A 7 year

This year is a time for manifesting your goals by visualizing them. See yourself triumphing and continuing toward your vision. Never lose sight of what you want, or confusion will reign. You'll be tempted this way and that, annoyed by gossip, and attacked by those who love you but don't understand what you are trying to do. Don't be swayed by them, or you will lose your opportunities and precious time.

Keep your head, as everything depends on your state of mind. Refuse to react to distractions, and avoid hasty actions or sudden decisions. A calm approach is the best remedy to the chaos surrounding you. You may have to move house without warning, but take it in your stride and make a calm, clear choice on where to go. If you are travelling somewhere exotic, be prepared with vitamins and medicines to avoid viruses of any kind.

Legal matters may arise during this year, relating to business, investments or house options. Consult an expert to avoid pitfalls, and, when you feel happy, proceed with confidence. If you have taken all the facts and details into account, you'll now be within sight of your goal. But watch your health, as the number **7** is connected with this subject for both good and ill. You might get fit and lose some weight or, conversely, suffer with some little grievance. This is a time for mental, spiritual and physical detoxing. Also, rest: take a vacation to the country, to a quiet location where you can think in peace. Let no one confuse you. You may have to wait, but you will know how to come out on top if you listen to your intuition.

This is an excellent year for study, research, writing and reading, and clearing out all the unnecessary people or ideas from your past.

An 8 year

This cycle brings the possible finding of a soulmate. If you're single, you could not have a better chance of meeting that special someone than now. **8** years also relate to money, so you may be caught up with an impossible workload and regard the arrival of such a potentially strong love as poor timing – and perhaps this is why it comes to you, because your attention being taken up elsewhere may be the best reason for someone's admiration. The love vibration you experience under karmic year number **8** may point to a future relationship prospect which has a lasting importance.

For those in settled relationships, pregnancy sometimes comes with this number, and it brings a very special link between the child and their parents. Or, you may experience a deep urge to study a subject that comes easily to you, though you have never learned about it before – a language, perhaps, or an artistic skill you were attracted to but never developed, but which you now pick up well. Even a professional subject that you seem to grasp quickly will seem more important to perfect than ever before. Partly, this is because **8** year cycles concern making more money, and dealing with the deeply felt past. There are huge opportunities for you in an **8** year, and you will want to be prepared to maximize them. However, you'll need to use good judgement and be efficient with your time management.

Many people feel pushed to the limit in an **8** year, because there is just so much going on. Consider, though, that the vibration of the number wants to find positive expression, so the more efficiency and determination you can bring to it, the better the chance of finishing on a high note. Don't over-commit your time or money, and be ready to acquiesce to others' ways of doing things. You need to be confident, but ready to adjust too. **8** is made up of two circles, asking 'infinity' of you. But this year, you can do it!

A 9 year

Your personal affairs all come to a head in a **9** year, and whatever has been insufficient, or unsatisfying, will rise to the surface and demand change now. It could be the fulfilment of many dreams, for this is the culmination of nine years' experience. Whatever is jettisoned was probably no longer of use – though this might seem dispassionate. Many friendships will drift away, but you have probably outgrown them. The strongest demand of you is a readiness to discard what will not be part of your serious future – and this can mean a temporary feeling of insecurity.

You will certainly travel in a **9** year. Even if a trip is short, or of no great distance, it will settle something in your mind. The more compassionate, tolerant and forgiving you are, the more warmth and generosity will come to you. This is not the right moment to start something completely new, but if events arise as a natural conclusion to what has gone before, this is a good thing. Your mind needs to engage with bigger issues, for selfishness or petty ideas will cause you unhappiness under this number. People will thwart you in your career and personal matters – and these obstacles seem to come out of the blue, and are beyond your control. However, if you think on philosophical issues and remain open to big ideas, everything will turn out well.

A **9** year can be populated with many friends and activities, yet can feel lonely too; this is a cycle for completion of tasks and the ending of what is not enduring. But this is the right time to see the fruits of your previous work. Be wise about where your destiny seems to want to take you. Your artistic and imaginative facilities are inspired now, and you'll begin to see new directions that you know you must investigate in the years ahead. You know what is missing in your life, or where you've failed yourself, and can now prepare for the new adventure that's about to dawn.

How to find your DAY NUMBER

Add the digits for the day of birth, and keep adding them until they reduce to one number:

EXAMPLES

14 February 1966	1+4 = **5**
23 August 1981	2+3 = **5**

How to find your LIFE NUMBER

Add the digits for the day, month and year of birth, and keep adding them until they reduce to one number:

EXAMPLES

14 February 1966	1+4+2+1+9+6+6 = 29 2+9 = 11 (a 'master' number), and 1+1 = **2**
23 August 1981	2+3+8+1+9+8+1 = 32 and 3+2 = **5**

Further reading

The Complete Book of Numerology, David A. Phillips, Hay House, 2006
The Day You Were Born: A Journey to Wholeness Through Astrology and Numerology, Linda Joyce, Citadel Press, 2003
Many Things on Numerology, Juno Jordan, De Vorss Books, 1981
Numerology, Hans Decoz and Tom Monte, Perigee Books, 2001
Numerology: The Romance in Your Name, Juno Jordan, De Vorss Books, 1977
Sacred Number, Miranda Lundy, Wooden Books, 2006
The Secret Science of Numerology: The Hidden Meaning of Numbers and Letters, Shirley Blackwell Lawrence, New Page Books, 2001

About the author

Titania Hardie is Britain's favourite 'Good Witch' and a best-selling author. Born in Sydney, Australia, Titania has a degree in English and Psychology, and also trained in parapsychology and horary astrology. With a high media profile, she regularly appears on television in the UK, US, Canada, Australia and South Africa, as well as receiving widespread newspaper and magazine coverage. Her previous titles have sold over a million copies worldwide, and include *Titania's Crystal Ball*, *Aroma Magic*, and *Hocus Pocus*. Her first novel is due to be published in summer 2007.

Acknowledgements

Many thanks to you, Nick, for the clear and brilliant vision; you knew what you wanted and, like a true and inspired **1**, kept mulling it over until a way was found. This is your baby. Also big thanks to Tessa, master number **22**, for your commitment to this magnum opus beyond call: only you and I know, Tessa, how much time and soul has gone into all of these words. To Ian, for keeping us piping along with a true **4**'s sanguine approach to such a long body of work, and to Elaine and Malcolm for the look – **6**s, naturally! For my daughter Samantha, thanks for some of your ideas which found expression in the second-to-last section: I love the latte in Soho while signing the author. Let's see! To Georgia, for work in the field on number **5**, my thanks. To all of you, my appreciation, and I wish you all LUCKY NUMBERS!

EDDISON•SADD EDITIONS

Editorial Director **Ian Jackson**
Managing Editor **Tessa Monina**
Proofreader **Nikky Twyman**
Art Director **Elaine Partington**
Mac Designer **Malcolm Smythe**
Production **Sarah Rooney**